365

Ways to Organize Everything

Emilie Barnes & Sheri Torelli

HARVEST HOUSE PUBLISHERS

EUGENE, OREGON

Cover by e210 Design, Eagan, Minnesota

Cover photos © Collage Photography / Veer; iStockphoto / Csondy; David Hughes / Shutterstock; Tom Baker / Shutterstock

365 WAYS TO ORGANIZE EVERYTHING
Copyright © 2011 by Emilie Barnes and Sheri Torelli
Published by Harvest House Publishers
Eugene, Oregon 97402
www.harvesthousepublishers.com

Library of Congress Cataloging-in-Publication Data
   Barnes, Emilie.
   365 ways to organize everything / Emilie Barnes and Sheri Torelli.
      p. cm.
   ISBN 978-0-7369-4421-2 (pbk.)
   ISBN 978-0-7369-4422-9 (eBook)
   1. Time management—Religious aspects—Christianity. 2. Housewives—Time management.
3. Home economics. I. Torelli, Sheri, 1956- II. Title. III. Title: Three hundred sixty-five ways to organize everything.
   BV4598.5.B36 2011
   640'.43—dc23

                                                                    2011030441

Select portions taken from:

15-Minute Organizer, © 1991 by Emilie Barnes, Harvest House Publishers, Eugene, Oregon 97402.

101 Ways to Clean Up the Clutter, © 2008 by Emilie Barnes, Harvest House Publishers, Eugene, Oregon 97402.

500 Time-Saving Hints for Every Woman, © 2006 by Emilie Barnes, Harvest House Publishers, Eugene, Oregon 97402.

Printed in the United States of America

11 12 13 14 15 16 17 18 19 / BP-SK / 10 9 8 7 6 5 4 3 2 1

Contents

Chapter 3: Organize Your Family

Chapter 4: The Joy of an Efficient Kitchen

Chapter 5: Align Your Time and Priorities

Chapter 6: Take Control of Your Home Office and Paper Piles

Have a time and place for everything, and do everything in its time and place, and you will not only accomplish more, but have far more leisure than those who are always hurrying, as if vainly attempting to overtake time that had been lost.

TRYON EDWARDS

A Welcome from Emilie Barnes

The role of the homemaker is complicated. Some women are full-time homemakers. Some women work outside the home or work in a home-based business. All women juggle many responsibilities in addition to managing their households.

Many of us who multitask like this have never had a good model for such a complex role. I've devoted my years to helping women become successful homemakers, showing them the kind of a home that makes a difference in the lives of children and spouses, strangers and friends.

This is not to say that there aren't men who have to play out this role in life. When I became sick with cancer and couldn't function for several years, my husband, Bob, had to take on this role for our family. He was so thankful that he had been raised by a mother who taught him how a home should function. It didn't take long for him to appreciate all the skills it takes to be an effective homemaker! It's hard work to manage a home. It is also important, rewarding work. Welcome to this gathering of ideas, advice, and encouragement that Sheri Torelli and I have created. Over the years and through our books, including our collaboration *More Hours In My Day*, we and our readers have become excited about the simple ways we can all make our homes and family's lives richer, lovelier, and less stressful. Read each chapter and put it into action. Put the ideas into practice, picking and choosing what works for you. And with a smile, let those around you know how much you love being the maker of a home. You and your family will discover the pleasure and comfort of being in a home transformed by the extra touches of love.

Emilie Barnes

An Invitation from Sheri Torelli

Am I still a good mom, a good wife, a good friend because I work outside my home? I'm completely exhausted, frazzled, and stressed to the max!" "I'm a stay-at-home mom and I still can't get my act together! What's wrong with me?"

In the frantic busyness of our schedules, it's hard enough to get dinner on the table, much less find time to organize our homes! My background makes it easy for me to relate to the out-of-control busy woman today. I've been there, done that! I experienced a time of total disorganization myself. I was working full-time out of the home, working full-time in the home, trying to stay on top of my two children's busy schedules, and constantly worrying about my husband, a firefighter. Coupled with outside activities and an active church life, I was on the fast track before it was popular. I needed help!

What I needed to learn was the art of homemaking. That's right—it's not drudgery; it's art! And that art is making a comeback. Women today are seeking ways to create order and beauty in their homes, but most don't know where to begin. And we can't do it the same way it's been done in the past. We no longer have the luxury of several hours each day to prepare meals and clean our houses. The frustrated, busy, overscheduled woman today needs hope, direction—a plan! We simply must be proactive and get busy using the small amounts of time we do have in an efficient and effective manner. I know firsthand how it can make a difference in the home and in the lives of our families.

I invite you to experience the joy and peace that an organized home and life offer. It is my prayer that you will use these quick time-saving ideas to make the most of the time you do have each day.

Sheri Torelli

Chapter 1

Why Get Organized?

Where and How to Begin

"I'd get organized, but I don't know where to begin!" This statement has stopped more people in their organizational tracks than just about anything else. We become overwhelmed before we even get started! Here are a couple of quick tips to help you get going:

- Break the big job down into small, manageable tasks. Write them down and prioritize the tasks.

- Do the worst task first! Once it is out of the way, everything else will seem much easier.

- Keep focused and eliminate distractions while working. To keep on task, set a timer for 15- to 30-minute segments of time.

- Take small breaks every hour to refresh and re-energize.

- Reward yourself when the job is completed. You deserve it!

The Way to Organization

Successful organization depends on many factors. In order to be efficient and effective as you go about organizing your life and home, keep the four P's of organization in mind:

- **Plan**—Planning is key to establishing success. Without

a plan we have nothing to shoot for. However, be careful not to over-plan. Too much on your to-do list and you're only aiming for failure.

- **Prioritize**—Determining what needs to be done is key. But after that you must decide the order in which your tasks need to be completed. This skill might take time to perfect, but you'll soon see the value of sitting down to determine what must be done immediately and which tasks can be put off.

- **Produce**—This is all about just getting started. Sometimes this can be the wrench in the works. We plan, prioritize…and it stops there. We must get going in a forward direction.

- **Play**—Rewarding ourselves after hard work is completed is important to success. It's much easier to plan and work hard if you know the payday is coming at the end. It makes hard work worthwhile. What rewards you choose are entirely up to you. Have fun!

Now let's talk about what hinders our success—the four P's of disorganization:

- **Procrastination**—Putting off just getting started is the main reason so many women are unsuccessful in getting their homes and time organized. It can be crippling if we are not careful. Keep starting. Even if you fail and have to start over, you have at least begun. That is much of the battle.

- **Perfectionism**—There is no such thing as a perfect job. Do your best, work hard and fast, but get rid of the notion that it must be perfect. It will cripple your progress.

- **Pride**—You cannot do it alone, so don't pride yourself

on being the only one who can do it right. Get help, delegate, and watch how quickly your workload diminishes.

- **Paralysis**—If you are not careful, procrastination, perfectionism and pride will eventually cause you to become paralyzed and unable to function.

Roadblocks to Organization

For many women (and men, too!), the desire for organization gets sidetracked by roadblocks that seem to derail their efforts before they even get started. Let's work on identifying some of the roadblocks that might keep you from getting started or completing projects that would make your home and schedule more organized.

- *Roadblock #1:* You're too easily sidetracked by other important tasks. Many times we get started, but something more pressing or more important gets in the way of completing the chore or project.

- *Roadblock #2:* You didn't allow yourself enough time to complete what you started. And you find that more often than not, you are unable to estimate the correct amount of time that is needed.

- *Roadblock #3:* The chore or project that needs completion is simply not something you enjoy, no matter the reward at the end.

- *Roadblock #4:* You know how to get the job done, but lack the skills necessary to keep it in order. Soon after you've finished an organizing project, you find yourself needing to begin it again.

- *Roadblock #5:* You are very easily distracted by nonsense and your personality lends itself to becoming too spontaneous. As soon as something else looks like more fun, you drop what you are doing and move to something new. Maybe you think you'll just stop to check e-mail for five minutes, but that five minutes can easily turn into an hour.

- *Roadblock #6:* You finally find a system or schedule that is working, but you find you are unable to stick to it until it becomes a habit.

- *Roadblock #7:* You schedule too much in your day and rarely finish your list, thus causing you stress and frustration.

The first step to getting organized and staying organized is discovering what it is that's keeping you from success. Only then can you move forward. If you have trouble even identifying what your roadblocks might be, this might be a good time to ask a good friend who can help you be objective. Once you identify the places where you need to change, the process can begin. You need only a teachable spirit and a prayerful and willing heart.

Setting and Keeping Goals

Getting organized is often a matter of sheer desire followed by commitment. Do you want to get organized enough to make it a goal? Do you want to set goals but shy away from them because of past failures to follow through? Or maybe you aren't sure which goal to set first?

With a little information you can learn how to properly set goals for your life. Proverbs 29:18 (kjv) states that if we have no vision we will perish. You are either moving ahead or falling back; there is no middle ground. We can label a goal as *a dream with a deadline*. Sometimes our goals are difficult to achieve because they aren't very measurable. We have goals such as "I want to lose weight," "I want to eat better," "I want to be a better wife," or "I want to be more spiritual." These are all good desires, but we can't measure them and they don't have any deadlines.

There are two very important parts to goal-setting. Goals must include:

- A statement of quantity (how much)
- A date for completion (deadline)

A proper statement of a goal would be "I would like to lose 15 pounds by March 15." This way you can determine whether you have reached your goal. But remember that goals aren't cast in concrete; they just point you in the right direction. You can always rewrite, restate, or even cancel any goal.

As you begin to set goals for yourself, write down the things you want to accomplish in the next 90 days. As you get proficient in 90 days go out to six months, then nine months, then one year. Bite off little pieces at first; don't choke on a mouthful.

As you list goals, consider each area of your life. For example:

- Physical goals
- Marriage/family goals
- Financial goals
- Professional goals
- Mental goals
- Social goals
- Community support goals
- Spiritual goals

An example of a 90-day goal for each of these areas would be:

- I want to do 50 sit-ups by March 1.
- I want to plan the 25th wedding anniversary party for my parents by April 15.
- I want to save $250.00 by February 28.
- I plan to enroll in an accounting class at the community college by April 2.

- I plan to memorize the state capitals by May 5.
- I plan to invite some families from church to a roller skating party on March 26.
- I will take the Red Cross fliers to my neighbors on February 14.
- I plan to read all four Gospels by April 1.

Notice that each goal states a quantity and gives a date for completion. Each goal is measurable. As you complete each goal, take a pen and draw a line through that goal. This action will make you feel good about goal-setting. You might want to write down a new goal to take its place for the next 90 days.

Emilie's Essentials

The Philosophy of Stuff

What is it about your lifestyle that causes you to be surrounded with clutter? Search yourself, your habits, your routines, your methods, and even your philosophy about stuff to see what might lead to all that clutter. I find that organized people have a calmness and serenity about them that disorganized people don't possess. Are you harried or distracted throughout much of your day? Does this unbalanced state of mind make your home and maybe even your work setting off-kilter?

Now think in terms of when or where you feel the most calm. Are there elements from that space or experience that you could incorporate into other areas? It's helpful to think about what eases your spirit. Too many possessions, activities, or worries start to crowd out even the best intentions. Strive for balance and simplicity.

Sheri's Secrets

Find Your Style

Since everyone organizes differently, there is no one perfect way.

But any project you start must be well planned. Gather all the necessary tools and set aside the time you'll need to complete the project.

Take the project one step at a time. A good place to start is to take stock of your stuff—or even just your *feelings* about your stuff. Answer these questions as you walk through your house, jotting down notes about the answers. These will help you set goals for the coming weeks. Enjoy the beginning of a new, more organized you.

- What area in your house causes you the most stress?
- Does your clutter or mess include paper?
- Can you set aside de-cluttering time without any interruptions?
- Do you have a friend or family member who can be objective about your "stuff"?
- Would they be available to help you?
- Where do you want to start? (Which room, closet, or cabinet?)

After you are able to answer these questions, you will be able to move forward. Always make any endeavor a matter of prayer and get ready to work!

Chapter 2

Inviting Order into Your Home

Does Your Home Say "Welcome"?

Take a few minutes to look at your home through the eyes of others. What does your dwelling say to people when they first approach it? "Welcome! Come on in. We've been waiting for you"? Or does it suggest that you are too busy, too overwhelmed, to create a visual invitation to your house? What does it say to your family? To you?

We all need a spiritual center, a place where we belong, a place where we can unwind and regroup and get in touch with who we truly are, a place that lets us reach out to others with graciousness and hospitality. We create this kind of home when we pay attention to a few details and invest our energy in matters of the heart. A home is where we nurture the hearts and souls of those in our charge. This responsibility is such an honor, and it doesn't have to be hard. It is our lack of organization or focus that distracts us and discourages us. We can change that as we empower ourselves with the wonderful gift of organization and as we get our priorities in order.

The best place to start is the very beginning. And in a home, that's the front entrance. Here are some ways to express your greetings to all who come your way:

- Sweep the walkway and the porch or stoop.

- Remove any dwindling plants and replace them with healthy flowers or shrubs.

- If you don't want to keep up with the plant care, place a wreath made of vines or eucalyptus on your door. This is a beautiful touch.

- Hang up a welcome sign or a sign that has your family name on it.

- Keep your entryway clean. Don't let your child's homework or the family's shoes take over this space.

- Once a week, approach your home with the eyes of a visitor…and make adjustments.

Four Tools for an Organized You

Do you ever look around your home or office and just want to throw up your hands in disgust and say, "It's no use! I'll never get organized!"? The old saying "Everything has a place and everything in its place" sounds great, but how do you make it work for you? You're busy! Your hands are full. Your schedule is full. Right? Here are four simple tools to help you get your home organized.

1. A To-Do List

Write the words *To Do* at the top of a piece of paper. Begin writing down all the tasks that need to be completed. When you finish each item during the day, relish the pleasure of crossing it off the list. At the end of the day, review your list and update it with any new items you need to add. If you have accomplished something that day that wasn't on your list, write it down and cross it off! Everyone's life is full of interruptions, and you need to applaud yourself for what you *did* accomplish!

At the end of the week, consolidate your lists and start again on Monday with a fresh page. Eventually you will want to rank your *To Do* items by importance. This added technique will help you maximize your time to its fullest potential.

2. A Calendar

Two types of calendars will serve you best. The first is a two-page "Month at a Glance" calendar. One glance will give you a good idea of the overview of the month. Details aren't written here, but do jot down broad engagements with times. For example, write down meetings, luncheons, basketball games, speaking engagements, dental appointments, and dinner parties.

The second type of calendar is a page for each day—"Day at a Glance." On this calendar you write down more specific details, such as what you will be doing on the hour or half-hour. Be careful that you don't overload your calendar and jam your appointments too close together. Remember to schedule in time alone and time with God.

Choose a calendar that fits your personality and style. Some will prefer paper calendars while others an electronic version. The right one for you is the one you will use.

As a guideline, allow 25 percent more time than you think it will take. If you estimate that a meeting will last one hour, block out one hour and 15 minutes. This way your whole day's schedule won't be thrown off if a morning appointment goes long, and you might have a few extra minutes to yourself throughout the day!

3. A Telephone/Address List

This list will become your personal telephone and address book. Design your own directory of information for home, work, and play. You might want to list certain numbers by broad headings, such as schools, attorneys, dentists, doctors, plumbers, carpenters, and restaurants. This helps you look up the specifics when you can't remember the person's last name. Use a pencil in writing down addresses and telephone numbers, since it is much easier to correct than ink if the information changes.

If you have a client or customer listed, you may want to mark down personal data about the person to review before your next meeting. The same system works well with guests in your home. Include some of the meals you served them, any particular food allergies they have, and whether they prefer coffee or tea.

4. A Simple Filing System

A great motto for any home is: "Don't pile it, file it." A simple filing system, when properly utilized, will make your home look like a new place! At your local stationery store, purchase about four dozen colored or manila legal-sized file folders. Colored file folders help you categorize your material and also add a little cheer to your day. These larger folders are more functional since they accommodate longer or oddly shaped pieces of paper.

Label each folder with a simple heading, such as *Sales Slips, Auto Expenses, Insurance, School Papers, Maps, Warranties, Taxes,* and *Checks*. Then take all the loose papers you find around your home and put them into their respective folders. If you have a filing cabinet to house these folders, that's great. If not, just purchase a plastic storage box to get started.

After you have mastered these four tools to organization, you can branch out and acquire more skills. Remember, though, to give yourself time, since it takes 21 consecutive days to acquire a new habit.

Are You Inclined to Clutter?

Are you a pack rat? We had to ask! Answer yes or no to each question. You get a zero for every no and one point for every yes. A zero is a perfect score (and probably impossible). If your score is 10, you might be a pack rat. You've come to the right place!

1. Do you often find yourself complaining that you don't have enough room or space?

2. Do you have things piled up in cupboards and closets or stacked into corners because there is no place to put them?

3. Do you have magazines stacked around the house

waiting to be read? Are you saving them for the day when you'll sit down and cut out articles, recipes, and patterns?

4. Do things often get lost in your house?

5. Do you think, "I'll just put this here for now and put it away later"?

6. Are things collecting on top of your refrigerator, dresser drawers in the bedroom, counters, end tables, coffee tables, and bookshelves?

7. Do you have things around your home that you haven't used for a long time or possibly don't even want?

8. Do you ever buy something you already have at home because you can't find it or don't want to look for it?

9. Do you often say, "It might come in handy someday"?

10. Do you have to move things around in your closet or cupboards to find a certain item?

Let's see how you did.

0–3   You're in pretty good shape.

4–7   You could use some improvement.

8–10   It's never too late, pack rat. However, I'd start with prayer. Philippians 4:13 says, "I can do all things through Christ who strengthens me."

Begin with a family meeting, saying that you have discovered a problem. Let them know that you need help and support from all of them to get the house in order.

Admitting this problem is the first step to getting organized. You didn't get to this problem point by yourself; surely the whole family is as guilty as you are. But *you* are the one admitting it, so let's start with you. You take the responsibility and work toward getting control. (Altogether too many homes today are controlling us instead of the other way around.)

Step one is to think of what area of your clutter is bothering you the most. Is it the top of the refrigerator? The front closet? The junk drawers? Underneath the bathroom sink?

Step two is to set aside a 10- to 15-minute time slot to take care of that clutter. Set your timer on the oven and go at it. You'll be surprised at what you can get done in 15-minute intervals!

Repeat steps one and two above with each area of your home clutter. It may take weeks to finish the project, but at least you'll be working toward organizing your pack rat clutter.

Begin to file away the piles of papers, letters, and articles into a filing cabinet or box. Remember: *don't put it down, put it away!* If you have a difficult time deciding whether to *throw* something away or *store* it away, put those difficult-decision items into a box or bag. Store it in the garage, attic, or basement. If an item is so important that you would retrieve it from the box, it should be kept. But if those boxes or bags sit for several months untouched, it's a sure indication to give them away or throw them away.

Simple Ideas for Organization

- Look at your home in a new way. Imagine the possibilities and potential of your living space. Move one piece of furniture. It will open up more ideas for your room.

- Simplify and unclutter your life by saying no to good things and saving your yeses for the *best* things.

- Any system of organization must be right for you. Whatever methods you select must fit your lifestyle. And remember, if it ain't broke, don't fix it.

- Determine and write down your priorities. It helps so much when you are deciding what and what not to do.

- I have found that my motto "Do the worst job first"

helps me get started. Once the worst is done, everything else is so much easier.

- Share your goals with someone who loves and cares for you. It's great to have accountability from people in your life.

- Visit model homes or take tours of homes. Write down features and ideas you'd like to try in your home. Then start planning toward that goal.

A Place for *Home*work

We talk with women from every walk of life and are always amazed how much we are all the same. We share many of the same issues, especially when it comes to getting our homes organized.

One of the issues that pops up frequently is that women do not have a place where they can conduct their organization of the home and family—a place to handle their "*home*work." Homework includes any type of planning or writing that keeps the home in good working order. This would include making your menu plan and shopping list, organizing your errands, prioritizing to-do lists, writing cards and notes to family and friends, signing paperwork for your children's school, and making phone calls.

Many times the reason we don't take care of these tasks is simply because we don't have a designated spot and the necessary tools to get the job done. We have the desire but nothing else. Here are a few ideas that might help you get started.

- You need a place to do your work. Choose a place where you are comfortable—perhaps a nice desk with a good chair and adequate lighting.

- Keep all your materials together at your desk or working area. If you must use an area that is already used for something else, such as the dining room table, get an attractive basket or plastic storage container and place

everything you need in one place for easy access. You
will be much more likely to get the job done if you have
everything you need at hand. Store it away when you
are not using it.

• Set aside a specific time each day you can devote to the
planning of the household. Get in the habit of doing
this every day and watch your life and household come
together!

Prepare a Place for Sleep

The bedroom is usually the last place we tend to change. Sadly, it
becomes a space filled with odds and ends, from piles of laundry to
library books to cold medicine. But it is the first place we see in the
morning and the last place we look before we close our eyes at night.
It is important to make it peaceful! Try one or more of these quick
and easy changes to update and freshen your bedroom. Once your
bedroom is in order, move on to your children's bedrooms!

• If you have a nightstand next to the bed, try mounting
swing-arm wall lamps on either side of the bed to reduce
the clutter on your nightstand.

• Keep the television and other technology out of the bedroom. No checking e-mail right before you fall asleep!
Technology is a distraction and takes up space. Don't
turn your place of rest into an office or media room.

• Make your bed each morning. This isn't good advice just
for your teenagers! If you take the two minutes necessary
to make your bed you'll feel better all day.

• Before bedtime, gather papers, extra books, phones,
socks, and bills and then deliver them to their proper
files and places. It will only take a few minutes and will
clear away clutter for sleep time.

- Better yet, keep the clutter out to begin with. Post a reminder note on the door or nightstand to preserve the bedroom as a sanctuary. You could also frame and display a favorite verse or saying that reminds you of peace and serenity.

- No dropping dirty clothes on the floor! Place used clothing in the hamper. If an article can be worn again without being laundered, take the few seconds necessary to hang it up.

Storage Solutions

Evaluation of the big picture helps you wisely determine how to shift items to create space, improve functionality, and increase storage for effectiveness and efficiency. A few simple additions to your home will help increase your storage space.

- *Hooks and pegs.* They come in a variety of styles and materials and are very practical for homes today.

- *Moveable shelving.* Shelves come in a wide range of widths and tiers. You create the size you need for your particular treasures.

- *Wasted space.* Do you have a corner that isn't used but would make a great space for a corner cabinet? Start looking for storage in the nooks and crannies.

- *Forgotten space* in the home can be turned into valuable storage. The space under the stairs can be fitted with pullout or standard shelving, and the areas around windows and doors are great for building attractive shelves to store books and collector items.

One of the easiest ways to get more space is to have less stuff! Clear out the old to make room for the new, or just to have the pleasure of open space.

- *Have a garage sale.* Remember…one man's junk is another man's treasure!

- *Give items away* to friends and family or donate them to thrift shops. Bless someone with items you no longer need or want.

- *Sell on eBay.* Let technology work for you. There are even local businesses who will sell your items on eBay for you—just pay them a small percentage of the selling price.

- *Take items to a consignment store.* Locate a shop that resells clothing and home furnishings. This is an excellent idea for getting rid of stuff you no longer need and making a little extra money as well. If you are selling clothing, make sure it is clean and in good condition.

Remember that by using small bits of time faithfully, you can accomplish great things.

Clever Closet Tips

Our closets can be a place of pride, filled with treasures, or one of the scariest areas in our home. Here are some tips to help get your closet in order.

- Use one style of hanger and get rid of all your wire hangers. They are not good for your clothes and will destroy the shape and fabric over time. Wooden hangers are best, but you can purchase nice plastic or fabric hangers as well.

- Color-code your closet and place like items together, such as blouses, sweaters, skirts, and dresses. It makes it so much easier to locate an item when it is color-coded and easy to find.

- Don't store your clothes in bags from the cleaners. Your clothing needs to breathe.

- When you purchase something new, something old has to go. This is a great rule that will help prevent clutter. Have your kids put it into practice so that it becomes a lifelong habit.

- Get rid of the clothes you do not wear. If a dress doesn't fit or isn't flattering, it doesn't belong on your hangers! You'll feel lighter and more put together if your closet is pared down to the pieces that fit the best.

- Try to use the closet for clothes and shoes only. Find new homes for miscellaneous items.

- Get shoes off the floor by placing them in clear shoebox trays. You can stack them high and still be able to get to the ones you want without moving a lot of boxes.

- If possible, put in a closet organizer with shelves and racks of different heights.

- If you have a dark closet, consider plugging a night-light into the area. It will help you distinguish colors and quickly locate the item you need.

- Consider placing risers under your bed to allow for storage space underneath. This is a great place to keep seasonal clothing and shoes.

Making Decisions to Clear a Closet

View each new season as a chance to do some pruning in your closet. Here are a few tips to help you out.

- Ask yourself, "Does this piece fit me well?" If you are not sure, try it on.

- Does it flatter you? Does it look as good as you remember? Ask someone if you need a second opinion.

- How does it make you feel when you wear it? If the answer is positive, keep it. Otherwise get rid of it.

- When did you wear it last? If it has been more than a year, get rid of it.
- Do you have more than one of the item? If so, let it go.
- Are you keeping it just because you paid a lot of money for it? If so, donate it to someone who can use it.

Get vicious and weed out everything you can. You'll have more room, feel great, and have space to put your new clothes.

Organizing and Cleaning Tips for the Bathroom

- Get rid of any health and beauty products that are more than a year old.
- Place large hooks across one wall in the bathroom to hang towels.
- Color-code! Have sets of towels, washcloths, toothbrushes, hairbrushes, etc. for each family member in their own color. When something is left out, you'll know who needs to put it away.
- Use turntables in bathroom cabinets. It helps save on space and makes it easy to locate items easily.
- A wire mesh fruit basket hanging in the corner or a tiered plate rack on the counter become instant homes for curlers, combs, soaps, hair brushes, barrettes, and more.
- Purchase a decorative toilet paper holder for a corner in the bathroom to hold several extra rolls of paper.
- *Cleaning the grout.* To clean the grout between the tiles in your kitchen or bathroom, mix up a paste of scouring powder and hydrogen peroxide. Apply with an old toothbrush, let sit 20 minutes, then wash off with hot water and a scrub brush. (Keep the windows open as you work!) You could also try a mildew stain remover

you can buy in the hardware store or supermarket and apply according to the directions on the container.

- *Whitening a porcelain sink.* First fill the sink with two or three inches of warm water. Add detergent and half a cup of chlorine bleach. Let sit 15 minutes, then wash the entire sink with the solution. Rinse thoroughly with hot tap water.

- *Cleaning glass or plastic shower stall doors.* Just put a little lemon oil furniture polish on a soft clean cloth and rub the doors clean. Be careful not to get any of the lemon oil polish on your tiles. (The whole problem of keeping the shower stall doors clean can be avoided if everyone wipes the doors dry after taking a shower!)

- *Speeding up a sluggish drain.* First run hot tap water down the drain, then pour in three tablespoons of baking soda and half a cup of distilled white vinegar. Stop up the drain and wait 15 minutes. The baking soda and vinegar will foam up, reacting with each other and eating away at whatever is slowing the drain. Finally, flush the drain with hot tap water.

- Consider hanging a small bookshelf to hold several books and knickknacks.

- Hang a clock in every bathroom to make sure you are staying on schedule when getting ready for work or an evening out.

- Group and store your makeup. Separate your daytime makeup from your evening makeup. You won't have to dig so much to find what you need!

- Put a utensil tray in a bathroom drawer and store your cosmetics, decorative soaps, and medications in its separate compartments.

- Place a turntable in your bathroom cabinet to house bottles of hair products, lotions, and liquid soaps. It keeps them organized and easy to locate.

- Hang a long, pretty ribbon in your medicine cabinet or inside a cabinet drawer. Hang barrettes and hair clips from this ribbon to keep them organized. If you have daughters, assign each girl her own ribbon color so the clips will stay organized.

- Consider installing a "stick-up" light in dark cabinets to make locating items easier.

De-Clutter Your Shower

Does your shower look like a garbage bag exploded? Is it a maze of half-empty moldy bottles, gadgets, soap pieces, old shower caps, and soggy washcloths? If so, help is on the way!

- Try not to store anything on the floor. This is where items are most likely to be forgotten and grow moldy. If you must place items on the floor of the shower, make sure to put them in a plastic container or basket. This can be removed to clean the shower easily. You may want to have one container for each family member that uses the shower. If space is at a premium, you will need to condense and use only one container for the whole family. Sanitize the container periodically in the dishwasher.

- If you have adequate storage space, consider buying bulk containers of shampoo, conditioner, and body wash. Transfer product into smaller containers to save space in the shower. Buying in bulk is a great money saver too!

- A corner tension rod rack works well with several shelves for storage. It is designed to fit showers of all sizes, and usually has hooks to hang wet washcloths and loofahs.

- If your showerhead is firmly attached to the wall, consider using a storage rack that hangs from the top of it. But don't overload the rack with too much weight and take a chance on it falling while you're in the shower!

Getting Housework Done in Record Time

Our grandmothers and great-grandmothers spent hours cooking and cleaning, but for most of us housework becomes a low priority when life gets really busy. However, dirt doesn't just blow away and elves don't appear at night while we sleep to clean up our messes! Wouldn't it be wonderful to have time to do things with family instead of spending all day Saturday cleaning, cleaning, cleaning? Here are some speedy tips for getting the job done fast and feeling great about doing it.

Start with collecting the right supplies.

- Bucket and mop.
- Broom and dustpan.
- Squeegee. Never clean windows with newspaper or paper towels, since they contain fibers that leave the glass messy. A good squeegee works fast and quickly.
- Knee pads (your son's old football pads work well for this). These great protectors keep knee work from becoming painful.
- Clean dust cloths. Old cloth diapers are great, as are clean cotton dishcloths.
- Carry-all tray. A must for storing cleaning items such as wax and window spray.
- Feather duster. This is a super item for moving small amounts of dust from a higher level to a lower level, where it can be easily vacuumed up. Invest in a good ostrich feather duster. You can purchase one at a hardware or janitor supply store.

- Pumice stone. It's amazing how quickly this will remove the ugly ring from a toilet bowl—just rub gently and it's gone. It also cleans ovens and removes the carbon buildup on grills and iron cookware, as well as removing paint from concrete and masonry walls and scale from swimming pools. Pumice stones can be purchased in hardware stores, janitor supply stores, and even beauty supply stores.

- Toothbrush. Great for cleaning the hard-to-reach corners of floors and showers and around faucets at the sink.

- Vacuum cleaner. An absolute must!

- Ammonia. An excellent cleaner for floors.

- Powdered cleanser for sinks and bathtubs.

- Oven cleaner. There's no better way to remove all the grime and baked-on grease from an oven!

- Rubber gloves to protect your hands from the chemicals in household cleaners and detergents.

- Scraper. Use the razor-blade type to remove paint from tile or glass and decals or stickers from the shower door. You can also use this to remove dried-on food—such as pancake batter or eggs—from pans after it's been left to harden. Be careful not to scratch the surface.

Fill your carry-all tray with the above items. It's ready to work when you are! And while you work, be sure to use the *speedy, easy* method:

- Put on some music with a very fast beat. This will help your cleaning go faster and take your mind off the drudgery.

- Go in one direction. Work around your room from top to bottom and from right to left or left to right—whatever feels good to you. Also start at one end of your home and work toward the other end. Don't get sidetracked by other messes; you'll get to them later.

- Before cleaning windowpanes, wipe or vacuum sills and wood cross-frames. Use your spray bottle with alcohol, squeegee, and cotton cloth. Use a horizontal stroke on the outside and a vertical stroke on the inside. That way you'll know if you missed a spot because you can tell which side the streak is on.

- Use your hair dryer to blow off the dust from silk flowers. Your feather duster will work well to dust off soft fabric items, plants, picture frames, and lampshades. Remember, we're working from top to bottom in each room, so you'll be vacuuming up this dust soon.

- After wiping clean your wastebaskets, give the inside bottom a quick coat of floor wax. This will prevent trash from sticking to the bottom of the wastebasket in the future.

- Change your air conditioner and heater filters every six months for best performance. This will keep dust and dirt from circulating through your rooms.

- Wipe off the blades of your window and/or room fans quarterly to keep dirt and dust from blowing around.

- Try to avoid interruptions; take the phone message and call back when it is convenient.

- Big question: Should you vacuum first or last? Last, of course!

Having the proper tools at hand helps immensely. Don't feel that everything has to be done in one work session. Set your timer and then work in 15-minute time slots. Work fast, but after each completed project treat yourself to a cup of hot chocolate or iced tea, put a mask on your face, and enjoy a hot bath. Then go to the garden and pick a fresh bouquet of flowers for your beautiful clean house.

Preventing Clutter *Before* It Piles Up

We've talked about cleaning up and clearing clutter. But let's take a moment to consider how to prevent this problem from building up in the first place.

Many of the things we buy are impulse purchases—items we really don't need but decide we just can't live without. One of our mottos has always been "A place for everything and everything in its place." If we follow that rule we can stay out of trouble. Here are some guidelines to prevent your purchases from becoming clutter:

- When you buy something new, something old must go—one in and one out!

- Do you really need it? Will you really use it? If the answer is yes, then purchase it. If no, don't!

- Do you have a place to put it—a place at home where it can be stored and accessed easily? Don't buy it if the answer is no. It will become clutter.

- Say no to other family and friends who try to pass their "junk" to you.

- Give your kids the number of storage containers you want them to have but allow them to choose what goes inside. Enforce your rule that when they get something new, they must get rid of something old. Teach them to have a heart of giving and compassion. If you model it, they will catch on!

Do I Really Need This?

A woman with 40 sweaters says, "It's hard to throw things out." Another woman has saved her plastic baggies from the supermarket and at last count had 320 of them! We must learn to sort and let go of certain things, or else we will need to build a warehouse to contain all our possessions, not to mention inventorying the stock of collectibles so we know what we have and where it's all located.

We often have things not because of an active decision to keep them but because we have not made the decision to get rid of them.

On average, people keep things several years after their usefulness has passed. Perhaps we overbuy and have supplies, materials, and tools left over. The things we liked years ago are not the style we like or enjoy today, but we hang on to them, thinking that someday we may use them again. It's as if we're obligated to keep them "just in case." Toys and baby equipment are saved because someday they may be used for grandchildren. We store things for our adult children "someday." Let's face the job of streamlining our possessions by asking ourselves some tough questions.

How long has it been since you used that item? If it hasn't been used in the past year it's time to give it away, throw it away, or store it away. Use trash bags for throwaway items. A black one is best so *you* can't see in it, *your husband* can't see in it, and *your children* can't see in it and raise protests about the items inside. Those broken toys, torn and stained clothing, and newspapers and jars you've been saving for "someday" can all go into the bag. Keep tax records (including canceled checks) for seven years and then throw them out. (However, keep home buying and selling records permanently.) Throw out most receipts, check stubs, and utility bills after two or three years. Use a shredder for documents containing personal information to decrease the chances of identity theft.

The irreplaceable items that you don't use go into storage boxes. These items might include your wedding dress, your husband's college letterman jacket, your grandfather's toolbox or baseball mitt, your great-aunt's lace tablecloth, your baby's first shoes, and other treasured memorabilia. Number these boxes and catalog the contents on a 3x5 card. This card should also be numbered and stored in a small file box. These cards are ready to retrieve if you need them at a later date.

Things you don't need to keep include old magazines (unless they could realistically become collector's items) or even recent period- icals. These could be placed in your doctor's office or convalescent hospitals. Junk mail is a big source of clutter and needs to be thrown away as soon as it's received. If you have a pile now, stop reading and take it out to the recycling right away! It's a great feeling, isn't it? But a new pile will return in a few days, so do it again. Fill your recycle bin—not your house!

When to Rent Off-Site Storage

One of the fastest growing businesses in the United States today is the storage business. We have filled our homes to capacity and are now paying someone to store our stuff! But when there is not a valid reason for off-site storage, you'll only be wasting your money. So when is it necessary or valid to rent storage space? Here are a few reasons to ponder:

- If you have accumulated belongings from a deceased rel- ative and cannot get rid of them for legal reasons.

- If you have moved from a larger home to a smaller dwelling and need time to dispose of furniture or belongings.

- You have become a caregiver for an aging parent or loved one and must condense their furniture and belongings until such time as they can be sold or given away.

- You need it for product/inventory storage related to a home business.

Beware of using off-site storage to accumulate junk you really don't need to keep. Get in the habit of keeping just what will fit in your home—you will find it refreshing! Use off-site storage only as a last resort.

Emilie's Essentials

Getting a Lot Done in Less Time

When you're getting rid of all the unnecessary items in your home, pace yourself. I'm not recommending that you start at 8:00 a.m. and work at it until dinnertime. Once you decide to transform your living space, you might want to tackle it all in a weekend, but you'll better serve your new vision and protect your personal sanity if you take time to create a plan of attack for each area or project.

You can do a lot in 15-minute blocks of time. For every 45 minutes that you work, give yourself a 10-minute break. Change pace, go outside, get some fresh air, walk around the block, get dinner started, vacuum a room—anything to switch gears for a while. When you return and once again focus on de-cluttering that area of your home, you'll feel refreshed and your perspective will be brighter.

Don't race through each day. Instead, try to work smarter, not harder. Plan your day. Pace your energy and skills through the day like a disciplined athlete getting ready for the Olympics. At the end of the day you will have achieved more and won't feel so tired and stressed.

Sheri's Secrets

The Art of Letting Go

A few years ago Emilie's daughter, Jenny, was visiting my home and helping me make decisions about some of my sentimental treasures. We decided to go through one particular cabinet of special collections to see if anything could go. She would point out a particular treasure and ask why I was saving it and whether or not I really needed it. There were several items I had absolutely no problem letting go of, but I wasn't sure about a few other pieces. Jenny gave me a great idea that I'd like to share with you today.

When you are going through cabinets, drawers, and closets and come across items you aren't sure if you want to get rid of, try placing them in a "treasure box" and storing them out of sight. Leave it there for one month. After a month if you realize you haven't missed the item or needed to retrieve it for something, go ahead and either throw it away or give it away. This was a great way for me to still feel in control and begin to let go of the treasures I no longer needed before they turned into more clutter.

Chapter 3

Organize Your Family

Family Conference Time

One of the most common questions women ask us when we teach a seminar is "How do I get my husband and children involved?" In our overbooked, busy lifestyles, it's more important than ever for everyone in the family to pitch in and help.

- Empower family members with job assignments. One mistake many women make is that they assume every family member understands his or her role. They never discuss their expectations with their husband or children. The family needs to understand the concept of family teamwork! Mom is not the only player in the family—everyone plays a valuable role.

- Try a family meeting that is scheduled on a regular basis. Pick a time that will work for everyone and then stick to it. Take the time to discuss the various aspects of the family and where changes need to occur. Discuss what's working and what isn't. Start by meeting twice a month until it becomes a habit. Institute weekly meetings if necessary. Family conference times play a valuable part in establishing harmony, respect, and pride within the family unit. Families that work together are successful, and children feel valued when they are allowed to be a part of the decision-making process.

- Celebrate success and milestones. As everyone feels the benefits of a smoothly running home, take time to honor everyone's participation. Have a game night or a pizza night. Plan a short family trip. Use this together-time to point out the importance of each person's effort.

Are We Getting Enough Sleep?

This must sound silly to some people, but it is a great question to ask yourself. When we and our families are running on empty, we struggle to maintain schedules, family time, cleaning plans, and our mental health!

Do you know how much sleep is enough? We must think of sleep like our banking accounts. The hours slept are making deposits and the energy spent during our waking hours are withdrawals. Here is an estimate of the amount of sleep needed by you and your family to be healthy and well-balanced. You might be surprised by some of the numbers!

Birth to 12 months	14 to 16 hours a day
1 to 3 years	12 to 14 hours a day
3 to 6 years	10 to 12 hours a day
6 to 12 years	10 to 11 hours a day
Teens	8½ to 9½ hours a day
Adults	7 to 9 hours a day

Young moms are often complaining that they can't get their children to bed on time because of the many activities and events in which they are involved. Sleep is so much more important to your child's well-being than an extra activity! Make sleep a priority and shift the other decisions, activities, and events to accommodate that schedule.

Another complaint I hear is how exhausted moms are. If you get your child to bed earlier, you will have some extra time to get things ready for the next day and still have some "down time" with your husband or time for yourself. It is not out of the question to put your young children to bed as early as 6:30 or 7:00. Once your children realize that you are in charge, bedtime will no longer be a challenge. They will be more refreshed in the morning after a good night's sleep.

And moms, you need to begin winding down about an hour before your bedtime so when you do go to bed, you will be relaxed and ready to fall asleep. Read a book or some favorite verses from the Bible. Sweet dreams!

The Never-Ending Clutter of Children

Children can accumulate more stuff than we can keep track of. And each piece of paper, small toy, or rock has special meaning to them. They struggle to part with anything that has some sentimental value. It is an ongoing battle. I struggled with the same clutter problems when my children were young. One of the most common mistakes moms and dads make is forgetting who the parent is. We need to take back the control in our homes, but at the same time we want to nourish our children's creativity. Here are some ways to gain control over your children's collections of stuff.

- You decide how many containers your children can have, and they get to decide what goes in them. Once the containers are full, they must get rid of something before they can add anything new.

- You can use plastic storage boxes, cardboard boxes, baskets, or any other containers you may have on hand.

- Allow your child to choose what is important to him or her and what they will keep. Start your own box with some of the books, clothing, and toys that your child has outgrown but *you* want to keep. Store these keepsakes in a place other than your child's room.

- Manage children's school paperwork with a system like we discussed earlier. Only keep the most important and meaningful pieces. By the end of their school days, you will have only one box per child instead of boxes and boxes of junk. And remember: what you are saving, you are saving for you. When your children grow up they will likely have no interest in that silly paperwork from second grade, but it will hold sweet memories for you.

- Consider making a scrapbook for each child with special artwork and school papers along with pictures. It will be a sweet memory after they are grown.

When Your Husband Is the Pack Rat

"What can I do if my husband is the pack rat?" Oh, dear. Even if you work hard to keep the home clean and clutter-free, you might be paired with someone who likes to gather, collect, hoard, and save everything. Is this your situation? If so, here are some helpful tips:

- Common sense needs to be the rule. You only have so much space. If you can't find it, you can't use it.

- Give him his own space (garage, attic, spare bedroom) and let him collect and keep anything that fits in that area.

- Assure him you will not throw his "treasures" out when he is not at home. Don't try to be sneaky: he is not your child, but your husband. He deserves your respect.

- Pick your battles carefully. He deserves to keep what is important to him.

- Offer to help him get organized if he is unsure where to begin, but remember to let him take the lead. Thank him for getting the job done.

Homework Tips for a New School Year

One of the complaints I often hear from moms, particularly working moms, is regarding homework. It seems to be an area of discord in many homes today. As the new school year looms, keep in mind these helpful hints for a smooth beginning.

- Have a special place designated as the "homework spot," preferably the kitchen or dining room table. Set aside a specific time that homework is to be done. For working moms, try getting the kids working at the table while you are busy preparing dinner in the kitchen.

- Allow no distractions while homework is being completed: no television, no Internet (except for school research), no iPods, no radios, no phones, no texting. Set the rules and don't deviate.

- Have some simple, healthy snacks ready for after-school hunger. Kids that are nourished will do a better job focusing.

- Have a "homework supply box" filled and ready for your children. It should include sharpened pencils, pens, paper, a hole punch, stapler, dictionary, colored markers, highlighters, a calculator, and a ruler. Buy supplies as they go on sale so that your box is always filled with the necessary items.

- If your kids are using the computer for schoolwork, try to keep it in full view so you can monitor their use and ensure that they're using their time wisely. This supervision eliminates distractions and problems before they occur.

- Keep your child's backpack on the back of the chair where they are working so that they can put their homework directly into their backpack as they finish each assignment. This way there won't be any excuses for leaving work at home.

- Be available for questions and input but resist the urge

to do the work for your child. Inspect their work for neatness and completion.

- Praise your child for hard work and a good job. Praise goes a long way toward setting the tone for success.

Don't Fight All Your Kids' Battles

This might not sound like an organizational tip, but it is! We are busy moms who use much of our precious time taking on the worries of our children. In doing this, we only encourage them to be anxious rather than resolve their problems peacefully and independently. We long to care for and watch out for our children, but you must be careful not to fight all your kids' battles. They need to learn to handle conflict on their own. It's important to intervene when a bully is hurting your child, but regular issues of sharing, compromise, and dealing with differences of opinion are a very different matter.

Your children need to figure out how to settle certain issues. This will give them a greater sense of control than running to you every time something doesn't go their way. We want them to grow up into strong, responsible problem-solvers. There is nothing cute about a 30-year old man calling his mom to complain about his mean boss or coworker! Learn to equip your children at a young age with the skills necessary to handle disagreements and arguments.

- Offer suggestions and monitor the overall situation but let them take the lead and resolve the conflict. It helps them to feel strong and capable and will definitely boost their self-esteem.

- Be sure to use drive time or dinner time to discuss what is going on in your children's lives. Their concerns will rise to the surface. Help them think through ways to resolve the tough spots. But don't take on each of their troubles.

- Trust your child. Each year, give them a bit more responsibility at home and also in their lives. If they say they apologized to another child, believe them. If they suggest that maybe another child isn't a good influence, listen to them.

- Pray with your children. Give them an outlet for all of life's trials and needs. They will find comfort as they learn that they can talk to God about everything. And when you aren't around them or cannot be the one to hear their needs, they will know they can go to God. What could be more important?

- Don't burden your children with adult troubles, but try not to shield them completely from your concerns. They need to see how you handle stress. If it is a financial concern, you don't have to explain that you can barely pay the bills. This will breed worry in them. Instead, discuss how it is an important time to save money wherever possible. Focus on the positive action and the remedy. Let them see you pray about decisions and discuss important matters with the family. They'll model this behavior.

- Organize your emotions. Don't let anger rule your home. When your children are causing trouble or are engaged in inappropriate behavior, take a step back, pray, talk to your husband, and talk to your child. Take time to organize your thoughts instead of letting feelings rule your decisions.

Start a Family Fun Night

Don't forget to plan for fun! It connects you to one another and breeds laughter, closeness, and creativity. Don't let the to-do list push out your chances to just have fun and hang out. Pick one of the following ideas for this coming week and get it on the calendar. You won't regret it.

And remember: family activities don't have to be expensive! Mix in activities that you save for with activities that don't require any financial planning. Each season of the year offers new opportunities and activities.

- Have lunch at a small and unique diner. Try different ethnic cuisines as a family and research that region of the world together.

- Write down as many blessings as you can think of. Share them together and thank God for all He has done for you!

- Spend an evening eating popcorn and sharing favorite family or childhood memories. Look at old photo albums or watch family movies together.

- Have a show-and-tell night for the family! This allows you to get to know one another and what matters to each of you.

- Plan a talent show at which each member of the family gets to perform a special skill. Maybe one child could sing and another child could recite Bible memory verses. Maybe you have a child who's a budding gymnast and wants to show off her cartwheels!

- Commit to a volunteer project. Get the kids involved in deciding on the cause, group, event, or even person they want to help. They will love this chance to give.

- Have a pizza night and eat on a picnic blanket in the living room, on the front porch, or in the backyard. Go around the circle many times and have each person suggest numerous family fun night ideas. Record these ideas on slips of paper, and then you'll have a great grab bag of fun to select from each week or month.

Save the Date Night!

In these times of economic stress and uncertainty, we are all trying to save money by getting back to the basics. But one area needs to remain constant...and that's date night. Just as we need family time, we need to set aside time to be with our spouses. There are a number of ways to keep the romance alive and save money while doing it.

- Instead of eating out, make a special picnic and go to a nearby park or sit by the ocean.
- Take in an afternoon matinee and save money.
- Trade babysitting with another family.
- Have dinner at home and go out for dessert.
- Date night doesn't have to happen at night! Consider a date *lunch!*
- Find an activity, sport, or hobby you can enjoy together.
- Have dinner by candlelight at home.
- Watch a movie at home in the dark! Pop a big bowl of popcorn to enjoy together.
- Play a game together or read a book aloud. Or talk about how you met and share sweet memories.
- Light some candles in the bedroom, turn on soft music, and share a decadent dessert in bed!

Teach Your Children to Manage Their Time

Good time management skills are learned very young in life. Remember, our children are watching what we do far more than listening to what we say. We need to be careful to model good time management as we move throughout our day.

Here are some quick tips to help you as you model good time management for your kids.

- Try not to always tell the children to "hurry up."

- Allow your children to suffer the natural consequences of being late. Don't bail them out. It helps to build character.

- Teach them to be good time managers by setting out what they need the next day for school the night before, such as homework, lunch money, sports equipment, instruments, clothing, etc.

- Give nonmonetary rewards for consistently getting ready on time or early for school. Make a fun chart to keep track.

- Set a timer for them as they work on projects such as chores, homework, or computer time. It helps them to judge how much they can accomplish in a set amount of time.

- Teach your children that we are being selfish when we are late everywhere we go, as if their time were more important than someone else's. Model good time management skills and it will catch on.

After you have taken time to set up chore lists for your children, make sure you let your child know when the chores are expected to be completed. It's not enough to give them a list to check off—we must set deadlines and boundaries. Kids need to know what is expected of them and when it is expected to be done. Otherwise, they will get sidetracked and before you know it the time for completion will have come and gone.

You may want to have chores completed before a certain time of day, before bedtime, or by a particular day of the week. Make sure your children understand what the consequences are if their chores are not completed. Maybe they won't be allowed to go to an event or an outing with friends, television and other electronic privileges will be taken away, or cell phone use will be relinquished for an amount of time. Make the consequences age appropriate and suitable to your child's personality. Don't take away phone privileges from a child who never talks on the phone. Younger children could lose toy privileges or have time-out in their bedrooms.

Give them a reminder one time and then follow through. It won't be long before your children become willing helpers.

Keep a Child's Room Tidy

I know it seems impossible for small children to keep a tidy bedroom. It doesn't have to be a losing battle, though! These steps will help keep your child's bedroom in great shape.

- Remember, you are the mom. You are in charge. That being said, you are the one who determines how much storage is allowed but let your children determine what they get to keep.

- Remember to keep storage at a level where the child can have easy access.

- Purchase a large mesh bag with a drawstring handle to hold your child's socks. Hang it on their door. They'll put their dirty socks in it, and you can throw the bag into the washing machine and dryer without worrying that the socks will disappear! This also helps keep children's socks separate from each other. You'll never have to wonder which child a socks belongs to again!

- Use large plastic containers for toy storage so that a child can easily put their toys away. If they are old enough to take it out, they are old enough to put it away.

- Keep clothes that children wear often in lower drawers for easy accessibility. Don't stuff the drawers, or all the folded clothing will come unsorted as they dig around. Put excess clothes in bins in the closet or in a spare closet out of the way.

- In the last hour before bedtime, designate five minutes

for pickup time. Play a favorite song to help this time pass quickly for your children.

Out with the Old, In with the New

Our children receive gifts during holidays and on special occasions. And if they have grandparents, they get gifts "just because"! Here is a way to keep these toys and items from taking over your child's room and your family spaces.

- For each new toy received, let your child select something in their toy box or room to give away to a needy child. Have the child come with you when you drop off these items at a donation center.

- Take some of the children's older toys and put them in a container out in the garage, basement, or attic. Rotate the toys back into their play space after the newness has worn off Christmas toys or birthday gifts. If they haven't seen it in a while, it will be like getting a new toy.

- Remove clothes that are too big or too small from your child's closet. Place them in large plastic bins and label the outside of the bin with the contents and size of the clothes. Too-small clothes are packed and ready to give to a friend or donate, and too-big clothes can be rotated into the closet as your child grows into them.

Try one or more of these ideas for yourself as well!

Children's Paper Keepsakes

Keep children's school papers for a predetermined number of weeks. Older children might need to reference their work for end-of-semester exams or end-of-unit tests. They should be responsible for the organization of their own school papers. But for younger kids, you can get rid of papers every one to two weeks. Keep several pieces each month in a folder, and at the end of the semester the children can choose a few special "let's keep" papers. By the end of the year, the file folder will consist of special papers, photos, and report cards. This lean folder can then be put into each child's own keepsake box, and by the time high school graduation comes each child will have a special box filled with memories.

Plan Hospitality Activities for Children

Start teaching your children how to reach out to others. Discuss as a family why it is important to reach out to others, emphasizing that people will know we love Jesus when we love others. Here are some great ideas to choose from as you organize family giving time:

- Visit a nursing home. The sight of a child means so much to a senior citizen. Teach them to smile and ask questions. Sing some songs if you can.

- Pack food baskets to be delivered to needy families anonymously before Thanksgiving and Christmas, or on any occasion you wish! Impoverished families often have access to resources over the holidays, but are left to struggle more during the other parts of the year. Make your family's commitment to outreach a year-round expression of gratitude and compassion.

- Draw pictures and make cards to be mailed to our military men and women as they serve our country.

- "Adopt" a child from a foreign country. Write and exchange letters and send small gifts if you can.

- Collect items to be delivered to local homeless shelters. Call ahead to see what is needed the most.

Short-Notice Guests

Have you ever had a friend or family member call and announce that they'll be coming to spend the evening—or that they just want to stop by to bring you a promised book or movie? Somehow these calls always come when you're least ready to entertain! Here are some quick tips for those short-notice guests. Remember to pay attention to the areas they will notice first.

- Grab a broom and give the front porch a quick sweep. Make sure to sweep away any visible spiderwebs!

- Close the doors to bedrooms, playroom, home office, and garage.

- Give any tabletops in the living room a quick wipe. Give the TV screen a wipe-down with a static-cling cloth to remove dust.

- Put kitchen clutter in the sink or dishwasher. Wipe down all cabinets and stove.

- If you have piles of paper sitting around the living room or dining room, gather them up and store them in your office for now.

- Give the guest bathroom a quick once-over, wiping down the sink and cleaning the mirror. Put out decorative soaps and fresh towels. Make sure the toilet paper dispenser has enough paper and close the shower curtain.

- Plump couch pillows and cushions.

- Spray a nice room deodorizer by the front door and lightly over the living room area. Greet your guests with a smile and a hug!

Emilie's Essentials

Bring Order out of Chaos!

God delights in turning our weaknesses into strengths. And did you know that God redeems our time and our tasks? When our house is in order we communicate better, solve problems more efficiently, and maintain stronger relationships. Organization begins with you. And remember the reward—having more time to do God's will in your life. Here's a thought for you to hide in your heart today: People before things. Relationships before projects. Family before friends. Husband before children. Giving before wants. God's Word before opinions. Jesus before all.

Sheri's Secrets

Beat the Boredom

Most children can name several activities they enjoy doing in their free time. In order to encourage their creativity, artistic nature, or love of the outdoors, sit down with your children, one at a time, and devise an Activities List. Make this time special by serving a favorite snack or drink and going to a special place to work, like outside on a swing, on a blanket under a tree, or in your bedroom on the floor, etc. Begin a conversation about what is happening in school, what they are enjoying, and places where they're confused, upset, or struggling. Then have them brainstorm, with you, activities they really enjoy doing at home. Let them write out their list and even decorate it with stickers or rubber stamps.

Keep this list handy on the refrigerator or a bulletin board. The next time your child complains that he or she is B-O-R-E-D, you can simply point them to their list and have them choose something they enjoy doing. You can suggest the activity or they can pick it out for themselves. Completing activities encourages self-esteem. And since you allow the child to pick the activity, it should keep complaining to a minimum.

Chapter 4

The Joy of an Efficient Kitchen

Accessibility in the Kitchen Is Key

One of the reasons we dread getting into the kitchen to cook is that items that would save us time and energy are not easily accessible to us. For example, the slow cooker will be forgotten if it is shoved in a back corner of a cabinet. Organizing your kitchen will make cooking easier and much more enjoyable.

- If you own a food saver, place it on a shelf by itself, at eye level, so the next time you need to pull it out to seal a bag of chips or store your leftover cheese, it is easy to retrieve and use. The same is true of appliances like the food processor, blender, toaster, waffle iron, and rice cooker.

- Keep items you use regularly close at hand and store like items together. Keep the coffee filters with the coffee, creamer, and sugar. Store paper plates, cups, napkins, and eating utensils together.

- To free up space in your utensil drawer, purchase a large, attractive crock. Place your most-used utensils (whisks, spatulas, and wooden spoons) in the crock and keep it near the stove.

- Try not to stack serving bowls, baking pans, or other cooking or serving dishes on top of each other if you can help it. It's much easier to retrieve a pan when you don't have to move the eight others that are sitting on top of it!

- Get rid of dishes, utensils, pots, and pans that have not been used in two or more years. They are just taking up space. Bless a friend with them, have a garage sale, or donate to a thrift store.

- Make sure you use the pantry for food and not a junk and clutter collector. Use the high top shelves for lesser-used items like holiday platters and serving dishes.

- If you have space above your cabinetry, use that space to display your vases, pitchers, and decorative serving bowls to free up precious cabinet space.

- Every time you purchase a new kitchen item, get rid of an old one.

A functional kitchen that has less clutter and easy accessibility is a kitchen where you will look forward to cooking. Remember, a mom shows love to her family in the kitchen!

Quick Kitchen Tips

- Once a month, place a glass with one cup of white vinegar in the top rack of the otherwise empty dishwasher and run the machine. The vinegar will get rid of odors and remove calcium build-up that can ruin your machine.

- When you finish a box of Kleenex, fill it with your plastic grocery bags from the market. When full, place it in your trunk. It will come in handy when you need a place for wet clothes, shoes, or towels.

- Every once in a while put the dish drainer and kitchen sink mats in the dishwasher to disinfect them.

- Place one opened box of baking soda in the back of the refrigerator or in a shelf on the door to remove unpleasant odors. Change every month.

- Keep your garbage disposal smelling clean and fresh by adding two or three slices of lemon. Alternately, you can dump a box of baking soda previously used in your refrigerator down the drain to freshen the scent.

- Keep a good, sharp pair of scissors in your kitchen and easily accessible. You can use it to cut fresh herbs and the corners off packages of dry mixes. You can also use it to cut up cooked chicken or pizza. Just put in the dishwasher to clean and sterilize.

- To pick up dry spills on your kitchen counters such as sugar, crumbs, or sprinkles, simply whisk them away with a lint roller! Glide the lint roller over those pesky crumbs and the sticky paper will pick up every last crumb.

- To disinfect your kitchen sponges and dishcloths, simply wet them under the faucet, wring out most of the water, and place in the microwave for 30 seconds to a minute. The microwave will kill any germs and get rid of that mildew smell. After taking them out of the microwave, rinse under water and wring dry.

- When cleaning out the pantry or refrigerator, set the timer for 15 minutes and clean one shelf or drawer at a time. Empty everything from that particular shelf and wipe it down. Throw away the trash, replace what belongs, and give away any items that you no longer need but could bless someone else. You may only clean one shelf a day, but by the end of the week you will begin to see a difference.

- Think of your refrigerator and freezer as another closet

or cabinet. Store logically, keeping what you use often easily accessible. Don't forget to use turntables on one or two shelves to store small jars of condiments, jams or jellies, syrup, sour cream, cottage cheese, etc. It makes locating and retrieving an item so much easier.

- Line your kitchen shelves with nonskid liners and a tea towel or dishcloth on top. The liner keeps the cloth in place and your pantry will look attractive and stay much neater. The cloths on each shelf prevent spills from traveling down onto other shelves. If something gets spilled, simply take out the cloth and replace with a clean one.

- Boil 1 tablespoon white vinegar in 1 cup water over stove. This will eliminate the unpleasant cooking odors that seem to linger long after the food has been eaten.

- It's not easy to remove burned or baked-on foods from your cookware. Try scrubbing the cookware with baking soda sprinkled on a plastic scouring pad. For more heavy-duty jobs, you might also try making a paste of warm water and baking soda. Apply the paste to the burned area and let sit for one hour, sprinkling warm water over the paste every 15 minutes. After an hour, scrub the area with a scouring pad.

- To line your kitchen shelves with greater ease, place the shelf paper in the freezer for at least a half hour before you use it. The cold from the freezer keeps the shelf paper firm, and it will roll on much more smoothly. The more smoothly it rolls on, the fewer bubbles and bumps will form.

Corralling Kitchen Clutter

The kitchen is the hub of the home. We need to see it for what it is really intended for—the preparation of family meals. It should not be the drop spot for everything from papers to coats, purses, backpacks, and clothing. Follow these tips to keep your kitchen both inviting and functional.

- Start by clearing off the counters, one at a time. Put away everything you don't use at least two times a week. Find a home for wayward vases, coffee cups, and rarely used appliances. Keep them stored in cabinets, high shelving, or drawers. Keep only what you use each week on the countertops. Fill a large crock with the utensils you use most frequently. Keep them close to the stove and the counter where you prepare your meals.

- After meal preparation and dinner is completed, store leftovers on one or two shelves in the refrigerator. Designate these shelves as the official leftover shelves. Teach everyone to use it. To prevent the risk of food poisoning, leftovers should not be kept any longer than four days.

- Add lazy Susan trays to the refrigerator, the pantry, and any cabinet where they fit well.

- Go through your pantry and get rid of any food you won't use. Give it away if it hasn't expired. Throw out all expired foods. This should be done every three months. Group like foods together so you know what you have and what you need.

- Purchase a large turntable for under-the-sink cleaners. Because it turns, no more backbreaking searches for exactly what you need. But remember to place only the items that you use for washing dishes on the turntable—dish soap, dishwashing liquid or powder, cleanser, and vinegar. All other cleaners need to be stored in a separate container for quick, portable access.

- Store extra sponges, rubber gloves, and other small items

in a small plastic basket. It will keep the space under the sink looking neat, and keep you from digging to find those lost items!

- If you store flower vases under the kitchen sink, use a basket to keep them together. Next time you need one, simply pull out the basket and choose a favorite.

Less is best, especially in the kitchen. Get rid of everything you no longer use. If you are able to easily access items you use regularly, you are more likely to want to spend time in the kitchen. Clutter, on the other hand, equals frustration.

Once you have your kitchen in order, don't forget to purge every six months or so to keep it organized and in top functioning condition.

Saving Time in the Kitchen

- Plan a weekly menu and base your shopping list just on those menus. Then add to your list those staples which are getting low. Make sure your list is complete before you go shopping; it will save you time and gasoline.

- Try to avoid trips to the market for single items.

- Never shop for food when you're hungry; you may be tempted to deviate from your shopping list!

- Plan your timetable for meal preparation so that your broccoli is not done ten minutes before the chicken and thereby loses its color, texture, flavor, and nutritive value.

- If you have such conveniences as a microwave oven or food processor, take advantage of them by incorporating them into your time schedule and menu for the week.

- Organize your kitchen and save steps. Keep your most-used cookbooks and utensils in an area close at hand.

- Save salad preparation time by washing and tearing

salad greens once a week. Place them in a Ziploc bag with a piece of damp paper towel, folded to fit. This will help keep the greens bright and crisp even longer.

- Learn to do two things at the same time. When talking on the telephone you can load the dishwasher, clean the refrigerator, cook a meal, bake a cake, mop the floor, or clean under the kitchen sink.

- Shell and chop your fresh pecans and walnuts while watching television. Then store them in the freezer or refrigerate them in airtight bags. When baking day arrives you'll be all set.

- Convenience foods are worth their extra cost when time is short. A stock of frozen pastry shells, for example, will enable you to make a quiche or cream pie in very little time. If you like to make your own pastry dough, make a double portion next time you make a pie. Make a ball out of the additional dough and roll it into a six-inch circle. Wrap the circle in plastic and store in the freezer for up to two months. It's all ready to roll out into a pie crust!

Cleaning Strategies for Busy Women

- When you are cleaning, remember not to clean what is already clean, even if it's in your line of fire. It wastes precious time and energy. If you scrubbed down the counters last night after doing dishes and haven't used the kitchen since, don't bother scrubbing them down again!

- Watch out for dirt! Be on the lookout for everyday items that are dusty or dirty. Money is wasted when we don't take care of the things we have. They won't last as long or work as well. Keep on top of your cleaning.

- When making your own homemade cleaners, use new

containers. Mixing chemicals with industrial cleaners—even in very small amounts—can be harmful.

- When loading your dishwasher, load the silverware into separate compartments in the basket, keeping spoons, knives, and forks separate. It makes quick work of unloading the utensils later.

- If you're making a meal and have ten or fifteen minutes to wait while dinner cooks, use your time in the kitchen wisely. Are there pots or pans you could clean now to save on dirty dishes later? Does the silverware drawer need to be sorted? Could you clean one or two shelves in the refrigerator or the pantry? You are already in the kitchen, so work smart!

- Buy large economy-sized cleaners and divide them into smaller containers or spray bottles. You will save a great deal of money.

- Use cleaning cloths and sponges rather than disposable paper towels. This will save money and resources.

- Learn to break down those big jobs into small, manageable tasks. The best time managers are those who use the time they have productively. Use time wisely—once it's gone, it's gone!

The Basics for Your Pantry

Every pantry needs to have certain items on hand that are basic to cooking. This list is not all-inclusive but gives you a starting place. These staple items are foundational to many meals and should always be kept stocked in your pantry.

Baking

Flour	Brown sugar
Sugar	Baking powder

Baking soda

Cornstarch

Chocolate chips

Vanilla extract

Spices and Herbs

Salt

Pepper

Cinnamon

Nutmeg

Paprika

Rosemary

Basil

Thyme

Sage

Cumin

Ginger

Oregano

Dry mustard

Produce

Fresh garlic

Onions (red, yellow,
 and white)

Lemons

Potatoes

Sweet potatoes

Fresh greens

Fresh fruit

Fresh vegetables

Pantry

Coffee

Tea

Cereal

Olive oil

Vegetable oil

Vinegar (white, apple cider,
 and balsamic)

Soy sauce

Rice

Bread

Dried beans

Chicken broth

Canned tomatoes (paste,
 crushed, diced, and
 whole)

Beef broth

Pasta (spaghetti,
 macaroni, etc.)

Syrup

Jam and honey

Peanut butter

Olives

Nuts (almonds, peanuts,
 walnuts, pecans)

Refrigerator and Freezer

Milk	Salsa
Orange juice	Mayonnaise
Eggs	Salad dressing
Yogurt	Ketchup
Butter	Mustard
Cheese (cheddar, mozzarella, parmesan)	

The Fast-Food Kitchen: 15-Minute Recipes

Tuna Melts

Toast split English muffins. Combine drained canned tuna with a bit of ranch salad dressing, sour cream, and chopped celery and place on muffins. Top with tomato slices and sliced cheddar. Broil until cheese melts.

Chicken Caesar Wraps

Prepare packaged Caesar salad mix and toss with some chopped cooked chicken. Add more Parmesan cheese and a spoonful of mayonnaise along with sliced mushrooms and roll up in heated tortillas or soft pita bread folds.

Chili Dogs over Rice

Cut hot dogs into one-inch slices and heat in a skillet with canned chili. Serve over white rice and sprinkle with shredded cheddar.

Taco Dogs

Combine hot dogs and salsa in a skillet and cook until hot. Serve in hot dog buns with chopped tomato, lettuce, chopped green onions, shredded cheese, and sour cream. Serve with tortilla chips.

Tortellini Soup

Combine canned tomato soup (diluted with water according to

package directions), frozen peas, and refrigerated or frozen tortellini. Cook until tortellini is tender. Sprinkle with grated parmesan and serve topped with garlic croutons.

Ham à la King

Heat together chopped cooked ham, bottled four-cheese Alfredo sauce, and frozen baby peas or green beans. Serve over hot biscuits or mashed potatoes.

Ravioli and Meatballs

In a slow cooker, combine fully cooked meatballs (can be frozen), refrigerated or frozen ravioli, and a jar of your favorite pasta sauce. Add ½ cup water to the pasta sauce jar, close, and shake; pour this mixture over meatball mixture. Make sure ravioli and meatballs are covered by sauce. Cover and cook on low for 4 to 6 hours. Sprinkle with parmesan cheese.

Turkey Marinara

Heat one jar of marinara sauce with cooked, cubed leftover turkey, chopped green onions, and chopped bell peppers. Serve turkey mixture over pasta or rice and sprinkle with parmesan cheese.

Easy Cooking Solutions

- When measuring sticky substances such as honey, molasses, peanut butter, or jelly, first lightly spray the measuring spoon or cup with cooking spray. The ingredients will come out more easily.

- When measuring food coloring or flavoring extracts, use an eye dropper for a more accurate measurement. You can add the liquid one drop at a time, mixing and tasting as you go.

- If you use a box grater for cheese, spray a light coating

of nonstick spray on the grater first. Cleaning will be a
snap!

- To remove the shell of your hard boiled eggs, simply
place the eggs in cold water directly from the boiling
water. They will peel more easily without taking chunks
of the white along with the shell.

- If you need softened butter for a recipe but it's frozen
solid, try grating it. Put a little flour on the grater first so
the butter won't stick.

- When zesting lemons, limes, or oranges, go ahead and
make extra and store it in a Ziploc bag in the freezer.
Next time you need it for a recipe it will be ready to go.

The Grocery Game

Here's a great way to save money for a special treat, some extra
cash for the holidays, or money to be used toward a larger purchase.
Once every three months, pick a week and decide you will not go
grocery shopping for that week. Instead you will make meals out
of what you already have on hand in your pantry and freezer. It's a
great way to get rid of items that have been there for a while and let
your creative cooking juices flow. See how many different and fun
meals you can make out of what you have on hand. You will have
to get very clever but it will be fun to see what meal ideas your family comes up with.

You can go online to www.allrecipes.com and choose the "ingredients" tab at the top. List the ingredients you have on hand and it
will give you recipe suggestions.

At the end of the week, bank your grocery money and watch it
grow. By the end of the year you will have accumulated a stash of cash!

Tips for a Neater Refrigerator and Freezer

Your refrigerator is just another closet, so let's get organized!

- Your best friends are plastic containers and bags. Lazy Susans are great space savers. Use them to hold sour cream, cottage cheese, jellies, peanut butter—and whatever else is cluttering up your refrigerator.

- Be sure to avoid "mystery packages" in your freezer. After a few days, you won't remember what you wrapped up in that aluminum foil! Label everything with the name of the dish and the date it was made. No more guessing how long that leftover casserole has been sitting there!

- When shopping, be careful not to over-shop. Don't buy more than what your refrigerator can handle. Food gets lost and will spoil more quickly simply because you lose sight of it. Crammed shelves lend themselves to spoiled food.

- When food or drinks get spilled in the refrigerator or freezer, wipe them up immediately. If they are left for days or weeks, they harden and become much more difficult to clean easily.

- Label all packages in the freezer and rotate often. Place packages in plastic bins to keep the freezer orderly.

- Resist the urge to pack items on top of the refrigerator. It looks neat and clean when clutter-free and is easier to wipe down—a few seconds instead of several minutes.

Storage for the Kids' Dishes

Special plastic dishes for younger children can be more difficult to store neatly because of their odd shapes and sizes. Consider storing them in their own cabinet in a large plastic bin or basket. Just pull out the container and pick out what you need.

Another good idea is to store the basket or bin on a shelf that is accessible to small children. They feel like part of the family when they can help set the table.

For sippy cup storage, make sure you have both matching pieces. Throw away any mismatched pieces as well as ones that are no longer in good working condition. You are not likely to find the missing cup or lid, and those extra pieces are just taking up valuable space in your kitchen. Store cups and their matching lids on a child-friendly shelf in a bin or basket. You might want to consider getting rid of cups that don't clean easily. They may be cute, but not if they waste time and space!

Quick and Easy Table Settings and Centerpieces

Just about anything you have lying around can become a simple, cute, or elegant centerpiece for your table. Taking a little time to make it special will make your family and your guests feel special too!

- When serving a special meal for guests, set your table a day ahead of time. This will give you a chance to visualize what you have in mind and see what it looks like once on the table. This will also give you time to make any changes you feel are necessary. Just eat your regular meals in a different location for that day. The kids will love it! This is a great idea to use for Thanksgiving and Christmas tables.

- If your meal is informal or outdoors, take a printed napkin that matches your plates and cups and open it up to use as a placemat. It helps to tie everything together.

- Turn different sizes and shapes of stemware upside down and place a small votive candle on the stem for a beautiful and creative centerpiece. Flowers (real or silk) or marbles underneath the glass add color and beauty. Arrange several different heights of glasses on a small mirror to reflect the candlelight, or arrange them in a line down the middle of the table.

- If you are having children in your home for a meal, consider setting up a separate child-friendly table. Use white butcher paper as your tablecloth and several mugs filled with colored pencils and crayons as your centerpiece. Allow the children to color on the "tablecloth" after they are finished eating. It will occupy their time after the meal, and the adults can enjoy conversation around the table without too many interruptions.

- When fall approaches, don't forget to use pinecones, colored leaves, pumpkins, gourds, or mixed nuts in shells to make simple centerpieces. Group the items together in a basket or glass bowl, or place a table runner down the middle of the table and arrange items for seasonal beauty and charm.

- When having a buffet-style get-together, here's the order for your table: Start with plates and napkins; then offer the main dishes, salads and side dishes, condiments, and silverware. If serving dessert, let your guests know that there will be separate plates and silverware for dessert later, along with coffee. If serving soup, it should be at a table by itself—bowls first, then soup, then spoons.

Party Organizing Quick Tips

Don't put off a gathering because you think it is expensive or too difficult to organize. Here are a few ideas to help you plan and carry out a party.

- Decide on a theme, event, or any occasion to have a gathering. If you plan in advance, you can watch for sales on colorful napkins or other decorative touches. The good news is that you likely have everything you need already in your home!

- Send out your invitations early.

- During the planning process set up a file folder to hold all your notes, recipes, RSVPs, information, and receipts.

- Write down everything that needs to be done and then break those jobs down into manageable tasks. Schedule tasks in your daily planner or on your to-do list and check off each task when completed.

- Do as much as you can ahead of your event. Pull out serving dishes, set up your seating area, set the table, and cook a dish ahead of time to freeze.

- Delegate, delegate, delegate. If someone asks to help, make sure to let them! Keep a list of duties others can help you with.

- If your party is not a formal affair, consider hosting a potluck. You can prepare two or three food items and ask others to bring a side dish. It becomes a fun time of sharing. You might even discover a recipe or two to use for your own family meals!

Emilie's Essentials

Experience the Extraordinary

I saw a great headline the other day. It read: "Never Have an Ordinary Day!" Now that's my kind of thinking. God gives you each new day as a gift. Take a little time to make ordinary things extraordinary. A note to a friend doesn't have to be ho-hum. Add a pressed flower for her to enjoy. Or try getting up a little earlier, and spend those moments getting ready for the day in a quiet time with the Lord. Make lunch or dinner a special occasion at least once a week. You'll be surprised at the reaction you'll get. Okay, so you won't be surprised! Today is a gift; take pleasure in unwrapping it!

Sheri's Secrets

Double Up and Reap the Rewards

Make your cooking time count! We've already looked at ways to organize your kitchen, but it's also important to organize your meals. A good way to organize your menu and to avoid the temptation of fast food is to start "double duty cooking."

Any time you can double or triple a recipe you will save time later on. Because you already have the ingredients and utensils out, why not use your time in the most productive way? Make an extra batch of macaroni and cheese and put one in the freezer, or prepare more enchiladas than your family will eat and save the rest for another meal. It's also helpful to label these dishes with the name, date, and some brief reheating instructions. A label might say, "Lasagna March 14. 350° for 60 minutes." The time saved will allow you to put great meals on the table in record time, and will create pockets of possibility for fun, relationships that matter, and a very happy mom!

Chapter 5

Align Your Time and Priorities

The average person wastes two and a half hours every day. Wouldn't it be great to have all those hours back in a single block of time? But in five- or ten-minute segments you can get a lot done. The key is to use the five-minute segments to accomplish a small task or make a dent in a large one. File your nails, make appointments, clean a shelf, throw in a load of laundry, or write a note to someone you thought of this week. One pastor provided a copy of the Psalms for everyone in his congregation. He suggests they use it when they have a minute or so of free time or "waiting time," as he calls it. Make your own five-minute file of ideas, articles, and to-do possibilities. You'll be amazed at what you can accomplish in these increments. It also breathes more patience into those waiting times.

The Benefits of Saving Time

Let's face it: Old habits are hard to break. The better you understand what you gain by altering your practices, the more likely you'll be to embrace the effort required to make positive, lasting changes! Time management is not just about keeping busy but about finding God's focus for you—choosing a direction and moving ahead to accomplish your goals. Success in this endeavor is one of the most essential skills a woman can develop.

Managing time takes maximum effort and realistic planning.

77

First, you must acknowledge that you have time—the same amount God has given to everyone. With God's help you must determine how to use this time. You err when you let others decide your priorities and set your schedule. Remember that by using small bits of time faithfully, you can accomplish great things.

The foremost challenge the busy woman today faces is not to orchestrate her life or to plan her year but to order each day, allowing for sufficient rest, proper nourishment and exercise, and a quiet time spent exclusively with the Lord.

To focus on what is really important, meaningful time must be assigned for vital relationships, especially with a spouse and children in the home. Work towards setting aside a special time each week for each member of your family. Put this time in your planner as you would an appointment. It will become the most important task in your day or week. It won't be easy, but the benefits make it worth the effort expended. And as you continue to work on time management with a positive attitude, you will find it gets easier and easier.

Time Wise

We've all got the same amount of time—it's how we use it that counts! As a woman, your biggest challenge isn't planning your *life*—it's making sure each *day* counts. My mother always said, "Good things seldom happen by accident." She was right! Whenever you catch yourself thinking, "I can do it later," stop and make a point of doing it now. Each moment of your life, once gone, is lost forever. Recognize this truth and reflect on how you can be a good steward of your precious time. Doesn't that inspire you to use your time even more wisely and purposefully?

Pray Before You Say Yes

Every request that comes your way doesn't have to be answered right on the spot. If you take some time to consider each activity before responding, you can change the way you fill your schedule. When the call or e-mail comes asking you to serve on that committee, to help out with the Christmas program, or even to have lunch, give yourself a few minutes before you answer. Pray for ten minutes. Work on a project, write some thank-you notes, or make a few calls. Anything but responding before you're ready! If we are laboring in vain, without direction, or only for personal gain and not for purpose, our labor can lead to worry and disbelief. Make your efforts count. Every day matters because you matter to God.

The Balancing Act

You can't do it all! However, there are many women today who believe they *should* be "doing it all." Our busyness has become a measuring stick, a way to compare ourselves to other women. The world doesn't rest on your shoulders. Learn to set boundaries and keep them. Bringing balance to our lives is simply a matter of setting priorities and sticking to them. Most women, when asked to take on a new project, do a favor, or join a new committee, group, or club, are afraid to say no for fear of appearing unable to juggle it all. But they're not sticking to their priorities of home and family. Is this you? It's been all of us at one time or another.

We must begin to change the way we think. The next time someone asks you to do something you know is beyond you, just say: "Thank you so much for asking, but it would be absolutely impossible for me to take on another responsibility right now." You don't need to make any specific excuse, and that way you are not leaving the door open for them to come around with a different approach. Sometimes we have the strength to turn a request down the first time, but when asked over and over we relent and give in. Here are some helpful ideas for keeping our hectic schedules balanced:

- Make a list of every commitment and activity you are currently involved in.
- Set a priority for each of the items listed: A, B, C, D, and so on.
- See where you might be able to eliminate a C or D

priority. The world will not end just because you are
not on a certain committee or group. You can see your
friends in places other than meetings or clubs. The peace
you will feel by getting rid of a commitment will be
worth it.

- Is there someone else who can help you carry the load?
Have an older child drive younger siblings to practice
or youth group. Ask your husband to run some of the
errands you now handle. Hire a teenager to help out
with the cleaning or yard work once or twice a week.

Once you begin to find alternatives for your busy schedule, you
will have a more peaceful home and a more rested you!

How to Quit Procrastinating

Napoleon Hill, an author who studied and shared keys to success for many years, perfectly defined procrastination as "the bad
habit of putting off until the day after tomorrow what should have
been done the day before yesterday." Do you struggle with procrastination? Believe it or not, this struggle often manifests in perfectionists. Perfectionists want everything "just so" and want others
to be "just this way" so that all will unfold as they planned. Perfectionists believe that everything must be done perfectly or not at all.
Here are some other excuses they use to avoid getting things done
in proper time:

- I don't know where to start.
- I don't have time to finish and I don't want to leave it
incomplete.
- I must deal with too many interruptions.
- I don't have the know-how to do it.
- My kids won't leave me alone long enough to finish
anything.

And the list goes on. But here are a few tricks that will help the procrastinator.

- Learn to break the big jobs down into small, manageable tasks.

- Invest in a digital timer. A timer will help you stay on task and complete a portion of the job at hand. Once your timer rings, stop and move on to something else.

- Use small blocks of time to break down the big jobs. There are many things that take only 5, 10, or 15 minutes when you are working hard and fast. Those precious minutes can make the difference in something getting accomplished and nothing getting done.

Overcoming the bad habit of procrastinating may take some time, but your willingness to give these ideas a try will give you a new perspective on your methods of completing important jobs.

How Important Is a Daily Routine?

We are definitely creatures of habit, but sometimes our habits need an overhaul. Even if your daily routine is more like chaos central, it's still a routine. Either you are in charge of your routine or life is in charge. Good or bad, how our day runs comes about through routine.

Routines are good for families. They help children feel loved and cared for and give them boundaries in which they can function. Adults can manage their busy lives much better with a functional routine.

A routine is nothing more complicated than a daily schedule of how you get things accomplished. The better your routine, the less stressed you will be. Here are a few ideas for developing a helpful routine:

- Don't overschedule your day. Have only realistic, doable

items on your list. Mothers of young children will be lucky to complete one or two extra items beyond their regular routine.

- Don't forget to schedule the things you do on a regular basis—making the beds, washing the dishes, tidying the bathrooms, etc.

- Put it in writing. Studies show that we accomplish 90 percent of what we write down. Once you develop a good working routine and it becomes habit, you will no longer have to write down each daily task.

- Use a schedule that is broken down into 15-minute increments of time. Busy moms will find that more can be accomplished in smaller rather than larger blocks of time.

- Do as much as you can before bedtime the night before. Spend ten minutes picking up, set up the coffeepot, set the breakfast table, sort the laundry, set out your clothing and your children's clothing, and write out your to-do list. You will start the next day less stressed and feeling more in control.

- Delegate, delegate, delegate. Every mom wants to raise responsible adult children, but the only way that will happen is to give them as much responsibility as they can handle at their age.

- Reward your family and yourself for a smoothly running home. With delegation comes rewards. Get creative and have fun. A family that feels appreciated is much more willing to help than one who never hears a "Thank you" or "Wow, I couldn't have done it without you."

The best thing about having an effective, efficient schedule is that routine allows for spontaneity. You will find you have the time to do the spur-of-the-moment fun things as well as handling unexpected emergencies when your home has a well-oiled, effective working routine.

Top Time-Wasters

We have found that although each person has a different method for getting things done, one thing rings true of most people: We waste time! This list of top time-wasters is not all-inclusive, but it will show you some areas in which you could probably be a better manager of your time. Below are five of the most common mistakes we see:

- Trying to do too much at once. Learn to prioritize your tasks.

- Failing to plan. Successful time managers look at the big picture in order to make a plan and set priorities. Remember: "To fail to plan is to plan to fail!"

- Being unable to say no. Learning to say no (gently and decently, of course) helps you maintain balance among your personal time, family time, and work time. (And it will help keep you from being resentful.)

- Putting things off. Don't waste time agonizing over an unpleasant chore—either do it right away, hire it out, or forget it! Procrastination is fatal to good time management!

- Doing everything yourself. You must learn to delegate certain tasks. You can't do it all.

After all is said and done, remember to set aside at least an hour of personal time each day to replenish the body and mind. When you do, you will come back more refreshed, relaxed, and ready to take on all you have to do. The time you invest will reap amazing rewards for yourself, your family, and your world!

Today Is the Day!

Resolve to make each and every day count. Instead of constantly anticipating tomorrow, live for today. When you invest in tomorrow's worries or schedule, you're missing out on what is supposed to be experienced, learned, or savored today! Have you ever spent a great deal of time fretting over a future obligation or task only to find that it was not that burdensome—but the weeks of worrying were?

Make today count toward your pursuit of a more organized life. Select one item and find an ideal place for it. Now, when that item ends up on the coffee table or on the kitchen counter, you'll know exactly where it belongs. Your quest to de-clutter your home can truly be this simple.

What to Do the Night Before

To be an efficient time-manager, try to do as much as you can the night before:

- Check the next day's schedule to make sure you know where everyone must be. Have each person check to make sure he or she has homework, permission slips, sports equipment, instruments, etc. Make out your to-do list before you go to bed. You will start the next day with a plan of action.

- Have each child pack their own backpack and place it at the designated area by the door going out to the car. You might even want to put backpacks in the car the night before.

- Set out your clothes and have each child set out what they will be wearing. No frantic last-minute running around looking for clothing items.

- Set up the coffeepot and set the breakfast table. Make lunches and store them in the refrigerator.

- Assign and delegate jobs to each child so they can be on board in the morning helping.

- Get adequate sleep so you are better prepared to face the morning. If you get to bed on time, try to rise 15 to 30 minutes earlier than everyone else to start the day. Use that time for quiet meditation.

- Put a load of laundry in the washing machine ready to start in the morning.

- Pick up for five or ten minutes right before bed. Set the timer and quickly pick up and put away clutter.

Escaping Morning Madness

For many moms, morning chaos is a main cause of stress. And morning stress can lead to a day full of frustration and anger. A stress-free mom is a happy mom! Putting the following ideas into practice will help ease morning chaos and allow for a great start to the day for everyone in the family.

- Get dressed and ready before waking the kids. You are then ready to navigate and manage the family.

- Stagger wake-up times for children. If you have kids that wake up easily, wake them up first. Or you can wake up based on age—oldest to youngest or the other way around.

- Load the car the night before with backpacks and sports equipment. No excuses for forgotten materials!

- Set out clothes the night before, down to the shoes. Older children can help younger children. No more complaining that a child can't find a favorite shirt just as the bus is rounding the corner!

- Delegate one morning job to each child. Maybe one child could gather all the wet towels and take them to the laundry room while another child feeds the pets. Change the jobs each week.

- No TV in the morning.
- Give each family member their own alarm clock. Teach them to set it and use it.
- Have a clock in the bathroom.
- Keep breakfast simple but nutritious, and require it.
- Check the calendar to make sure you know where everyone must be during the day.
- Pray for your children and the day ahead as you are leaving. Send each one off with a hug and a smile!

Throw Your Hat over the Fence

Have you ever heard the expression "Just throw your hat over the fence"? It means that once you've made the first step, you're committed to taking the next. After all, if you throw your hat over the fence you have to get it back. Is it time for you to commit to getting organized? Sometimes, that's what it takes to get started.

Think about a project or some area of clutter you have been putting off organizing. Why not "throw your hat over the fence" and commit yourself to getting started? You'll never get around to finishing it if you never take the first steps. Here are a few ideas to get yourself going and "throw your hat over the fence!"

- Invite family or friends over for a visit to see the new craft room or your newly painted living room. By setting a date you will be motivated to get the job done.

- Visualize the end. Try to imagine what the project will look like once it's completed, and how you'll feel about the task once the burden of it is off your shoulders. Many times that is all it takes to get started.

- Think back to the last time you completed a project

successfully. Use that success to help motivate you to success in this one.

- Find a friend who is successful in both beginning and completing projects. Ask how she organizes her time and how she gets motivated to start a new task.

- Make yourself accountable to another person. This could be a spouse, parent, or close friend. Ask your accountability partner to check in with you periodically as you work on the project, and be honest in what you've accomplished.

Gaining Perspective

There is no one way to get organized. You have be aware of your own personality, inner clock, season of life, and daily routines as you decide what method will work best to get your home and life in order.

Try looking at your home or office as a huge assignment which demands that work be broken down into smaller, manageable tasks. Break your work that needs to be completed into projects. Try to keep the projects achievable in 15-minute increments of time if possible. For example, in 15 minutes you can clean the top of the refrigerator. Take everything off the top of the fridge and wipe it off with a damp cloth and cleaning solution. Put back only what belongs there. Take the remnants and divide into three piles: throw away, give away, and put away. Throw out the trash, put the giveaway items in the trunk of your car to take to a thrift store, and put the rest of the items back where they belong. One project down!

At the office, you may need to clean out a drawer or file cabinet. Use the same process, giving yourself a reward for completing the job. If it is a project at work, reward yourself with lunch out with a friend. At home, treat yourself to a bubble bath by candlelight or a quick cup of coffee with a friend or neighbor. This will help motivate you to continue developing your "project planner."

Keep a list of projects that need to get done in your planner or in a file folder. When you have some downtime, you can quickly tackle a project and cross it off your list!

Simple Time-Savers

When we find ways to save time here and there, we end up with more breathing room and the space to care for our families with greater patience, attention, and preparation. Here are three sure-fire ways to save time! And with the time you save, maybe spare a few minutes to consider even more ways to live efficiently and embrace life more fully.

We all have the same amount of time each day. What we do with it is completely up to us. Think about the following:

- Shop from home using your computer or catalogs. Just about anything you can think of is available online or from a catalog. Online shopping is safe and easy. Remember: Time is money.

- Opt for delivery. The money and time saved by having items delivered is tremendous. When you add up the time, the gas, and the stress, the money you pay for delivery will be well worth it.

- Don't set your clocks at home or in the car five or ten minutes ahead. You will remember you have the extra time so the perceived benefit is lost. Just by wearing a watch and keeping it set to the correct time you can help yourself stay on schedule.

- Do errands on the way to or from work. Delegate errands whenever possible.

- Get help from family members and delegate jobs and responsibilities at home.

- Get up half an hour earlier.

- Don't be distracted by the television or computer. Keep them off. When you are watching TV or working on the computer, set a timer to monitor how much time you spend.

- Cook more than one meal at a time.

- Eliminate items on your to-do list that aren't a priority.

- Learn to say no.

- Take time to relax, plan, and dream.

Make a Cleaning Date

Make an appointment with yourself for your next cleaning/organization project. Write the time on your calendar just as though it were a business or doctor's appointment. This will make you keep the date, help you get started, and provide the motivation to stick to your plans.

When you put the appointment on your calendar, protect it like you would a top priority. Don't be tempted to cancel it when a better offer comes your way. You don't do that to your friends or to your work commitments, so don't do it to yourself. When you have a project scheduled on an upcoming evening, afternoon, or weekend, spend some time before that appointment considering how you'll tackle it. It becomes a great joy to follow through on your promises to yourself to make your home and life better.

Prevent Interruptions

Most people are interrupted at least once every five minutes. If this is true for you, analyze what it is that's most often causing those interruptions. You and your situation are unique, and the things that disrupt your day are different than the things that disrupt anyone else's. If you haven't studied this loss of time, become aware of it. You will be amazed at how much time is whittled away by these interruptions and disturbances.

Consider ways in which you could safeguard your time. There's nothing wrong with telling people you can see them at 9:30, 12:15, or 6:40 exactly. Even family members can be taught not to interrupt. Maybe you cause the interruptions by insisting on checking e-mail every few minutes or answering your cell phone even when you are in the middle of something. If you don't respect your time, others certainly won't.

Take Time for What Matters Most

What do you do when someone in your life is overwhelmed by a deadline and asks for your help at the last minute? Do you stop your important project to help them? There really is more than one answer to this problem, but choosing the correct one is sometimes not so evident.

Your dilemma really boils down to one thing: priorities. But it involves more than just the task of deciding which endeavor is more important. It's about people and relationships. So the next time you are confronted with a similar situation, stop and ask yourself a few questions to help you make the right choice.

- How much time will I lose if I stop and work on something different?
- Would a break be a refreshing change of pace?
- What is the worst-case scenario if I say no?
- When evaluating this situation, do I find it happening more often than not?
- Am I helping or hurting the situation by getting involved?
- Can anyone else be enlisted to help or am I the only person that can assist in this situation?
- Am I enabling the person requesting my help to continue following a path of bad habits and poor time management?

- Will the neglect of my project cause a problem for some-one else?

- Might there be an alternative solution that could defer my help temporarily until I can complete my work?

- Is my relationship to the person requesting my help more important than the project I am involved in?

Remember, poor planning on one person's part does not consti-tute an emergency for another. But at the same time, grace extended can be a true gift from God. Evaluate the situation and do what is best for all involved.

Secrets to Productivity

It's a fact...some people are just more productive than others. They just seem to know how best to get more done in less time. What's their secret?

- Have a plan. Planning ahead eliminates surprises.

- Make sure you have everything you need before starting a project. It will save time if you don't have to stop to purchase or search for something you need to complete your work.

- Count the cost. Calculate the time and money invest-ment before you begin. This will eliminate getting started and having to stop midway due to time or money constraints.

- Be well rested before tackling a big project. Good rest is essential to success.

- Eliminate distractions as much as possible. Let the answering machine take calls or get a sitter.

- Start early, work fast, and set a timer to stay on task. Take a quick five- to ten-minute break for every hour you are working.

When the job is done, reward yourself with a lunch out with a friend, a shopping trip, an afternoon at the park with your children, or whatever you really enjoy!

Emilie's Essentials

Best for Last

One of the basic principles I share in my organizational seminars is "Do the worst first." Once you complete the worst part of the project, everything else is easy. This is also a great rule to follow if you find yourself procrastinating. We all dread the worst—that's why it's best to get it out of the way in the beginning of the project!

When you enter a room with plans to clean it, determine which of the projects you dread most. Take a minute to break down the whole job into smaller tasks. Now choose the worst of the small tasks and do that one first. You will learn three things about this "Do the worst first" rule:

- It didn't take you as long as you thought.
- It wasn't as bad as you thought it would be.
- It made room for the best things!

Sheri's Secrets

Order and Happiness Go Together

It has been written that the true secret to happiness is not in getting more, but in wanting less. If that is true (and I believe it is), then we may have stumbled on the secret to getting our lives in order. We discover real joy in contentment and even greater joy in getting rid of useless junk. We can do this in several different ways:

- Don't spend too much time window-shopping for entertainment. Save your shopping for the times when you have a need or an occasion to shop.
- Avoid reading all the latest fashion and home décor

magazines. They only cause you to want more than you really need or have room to store.

- Always keep in the back of your mind the thought that you are not taking anything with you.

- Become a "gifter" of stuff that has been admired by others and is only collecting dust at your house. If a particular collection or piece of furniture is no longer your style, give it to someone who can give it new life.

- Learn to turn loose the death grip you have on your possessions and put your arms around the real treasures that matter—your relationships.

Things come and go, styles come and go, everything comes and goes. But God is the same yesterday, today, and forever! We must place a high priority on the things that are eternal and lasting—people and relationships. Those are the only treasures you can take to heaven! Cherish those flesh and blood "belongings" above all, and learn to be content in wanting less!

Chapter 6

Take Control of Your Home Office and Paper Piles

What to Do with Those Piles of Papers

Every day we make decisions about paper—from personal mail to children's papers, newspapers to magazines, junk mail to Sunday school papers. We must sort through mountains of paper accumulated from day to day, week to week, and month to month. A woman who attended one of the More Hours in My Day seminars shared that she finally had to hire someone to help her organize her papers. A former schoolteacher, she had acquired volumes of miscellaneous papers. She and her helper worked three hours a day, five days a week, for three months during summer vacation just organizing paper—a total of 180 hours each!

A lot of time and expense can be avoided if paper is dealt with when it arrives. Rather than stacking it on counters, appliance tops, tables, dressers, or even on the floor until it takes up nearly every empty space in our homes, we need to file or dispose of paper as soon as it is received.

Another lady confessed that she couldn't use her dining room table without a major paper transfer before entertaining company. Still another woman shared that her husband had threatened, "It's either me or the papers that go." Needless to say, she began a major paper-filing program and quickly got the paper epidemic under control.

Paper disorganization often begins in subtle ways. With only insurance policies, checking account statements, canceled checks, car registrations, apartment rental agreements, birth certificates, a marriage license, diplomas, and a few other miscellaneous papers, a person often reasons that a full-fledged filing system is not necessary. Thus the file often consists of merely a cardboard shoebox or metal, fireproof box which can easily be stored away on a closet shelf.

As the years go by, however, there are "his" papers, "her" papers, appliance warranties, and instruction booklets on the television, the toaster, and the lawn mower (along with other gadgets too numerous to mention). The result is paper chaos.

Don't despair. Help is on the way. Here are six simple steps to effective paper-management.

- Schedule set times for sorting through papers.
- Collect materials you will need to help you get organized.
    - Metal filing cabinet or file boxes
    - Paper grocery bags, for recycling
    - File folders (try brightly colored folders, but plain manila will do)
    - Black felt marking pen
- Begin.
    - Start with whatever room annoys you the most. Work your way through every pile of paper, making sure to go through drawers and check closets as well. Then move on to rooms where other papers have accumulated. Continue at set times until your project is completed.
- Toss.
    - Perhaps you have lots of articles, recipes, or children's

school papers and artwork which you have been saving for that far-off "someday." In each category, choose five pieces to keep and recycle the rest. Try not to be too sentimental.

- Be determined. Make decisions. Throw away the clutter.

- Keep paper-saving to a minimum. Put the throw-away papers into bags and carry them out to the recycling. Don't wait. It's a good feeling!

- Don't get bogged down rereading old letters, recipes, or articles. It's easy to spend too much time reminiscing and get sidetracked from your purpose.

- Keep legal papers a minimum of seven years.

- If you have trouble determining what to throw away, ask a friend to help you make some of those decisions. Friends tend to be more objective and you can return the favor when they discover how organized you are.

- File.

  - Keep your filing system as simple as possible. If it is too detailed and complex, you may be easily discouraged.

  - Categorize the papers you want to save (magazine articles, Bible study notes, family information, IRS papers, bank statements/canceled checks, charge accounts, utilities, and investments).

  - Label the file folders with a felt pen.

  - Within each category, mark a folder or envelope for each separate account. For example, place water, gasoline, and telephone bills in the utilities folder. In the insurance folder, it is helpful to designate separate envelopes for life, health, car, and house insurance.

- Label a folder for each member of the family. These can be used for keeping health records, report cards, notes, drawings, awards, and other special remembrances.

- Other suggestions for categories: vacation possibilities, Christmas card lists, home improvement ideas, warranties, instruction booklets, photos/negatives, and car/home repair receipts.

- File papers in appropriate folders. *Do it at the time they are received and/or paid.* Take special care to file away your check stubs, paid receipts, and other budget records on the day you receive your paycheck.

- Place files in cabinet or boxes.

• Store.

- Store files (cabinets or boxes) in a closet, garage, attic, or some other area that is out of sight, yet easily accessible.

- Be sure to label the file boxes. I use a 3x5 card stapled on the end of the box with the contents written on the card ("Medical Records, 2008–2011," for example). If I empty the box at a later date, I can easily tear off the card and replace it with a blank one, or use the box for other items.

Remember, you need to start right where you are—tackling your own mountains of paper by filing and storing the information you want and disposing of the clutter that depresses and discourages you.

When you get to the bottom of the "put away" pile, you will probably find many loose items of papers and records that need some type of storage for quick retrieval. This is where your file folders come in handy. Label the folders with the following headings and then place each paper or receipt in the corresponding folder:

Insurance Papers
- Auto
- Health
- Homeowner's

Homeowner Papers
- Escrow papers
- Tax records (for current year)

Receipts
- Auto repairs
- Major purchases

Store these folders in a metal file cabinet or a storage box. If possible, keep these boxes near the office area in your home. Close accessibility to these files will save you extra footsteps when you need to get to them.

Give your young children storage boxes, file cards, and file folders to help them keep their rooms organized. This provides an excellent model for their future personal organization. Just think of your satisfaction when a member of your family comes to you and asks where something is and you pull out your box, flip through your cards, and tell him or her to look in Box 5, which is located under the attic stairs!

Reduce! Reduce!

Every day we must make decisions about paper. If you leave a pile of paper and go into another room to take care of something, when you return that pile of paper will have had "babies" all over your home! Here are a few quick tips to handle the sometimes overwhelming paper clutter in your home.

- When the mail arrives, designate one person to take care of processing it. Recycle or shred what you must get rid of immediately.

- File your household bills in one folder marked "House-hold Bills–Month, Year." After paying the bills, file the "paid stubs" back in the same folder and place the entire folder in your file cabinet. Any time you might need to retrieve an item, you will need to look for it by date first. Unless the items in this folder are tax deductible, save them for no more than one year. Shred the folder contents and start over.

- Consider sharing magazine subscriptions with a friend. If you trade the magazines back and forth, you'll be less likely to keep them lying around the house.

- Have a "reading" file folder handy on your counter to place all the magazines, catalogs, and newsletters that you don't have time to read as the mail arrives. Each time you leave to run errands or drive on a trip, grab the folder and take it with you to read when you find yourself waiting. When you find something of interest, tear it out immediately. You will not remember next week what you were saving the magazine for.

- Store computer manuals and software and appliance manuals in accordion files. Keep the accordion file near your computer for easy retrieval.

- Buy a flat basket to organize newspapers and old magazines for recycling.

- Provide secure protection for your important papers in a lockbox or safe.

- Get rid of extra paper. Almost 80 percent of the paper in your home is never looked at again.

Filing Tips

When filing at home try one or more of these hints and helps:

- When you remove a file folder from the cabinet, insert a piece of paper to mark the spot. Re-filing is a snap!

- When filing paperwork, place the newest piece of paper in the front of the folder. The most recent paper will always be in the front and easier to locate.

- Purge your files at least once a quarter or twice a year.

- Don't overstuff your filing cabinets or drawers. Leave room for growth. It makes retrieving files easier.

- Set aside five minutes a day or every other day to file. You will stay right on top of your paperwork and paper clutter will be cut to a minimum.

Getting Office Clutter Under Control

We have all experienced the slippery slope of office clutter. If you work out of the home, run a home-based business, or have an area dedicated to your files and papers for your family, office clutter can accumulate and absorb much of your time and energy. Have you ever given up on returning an item because you just couldn't find where you had stuffed that receipt? Try a few of these hints to keep clutter under control and become more productive.

- A place for everything and everything in its place. Every item in your office needs a place to call home. You will find yourself much more productive if you are not constantly moving things around to find space to work.

- Keep your recycling bin and shredder within reach. As soon as you know you can get rid of a piece of paper, either toss it or shred it. Remember, 80 percent of all paper we accumulate is never used again. Try to handle paper one time.

- When going through piles of paper, start with the most recent and work backwards, not the other way around.

- Remember: you can be neat and still disorganized. Make sure all your files and boxes are easily accessible and organized for quick retrieval of papers and information.

- Get rid of anything that doesn't work or that you don't use. This includes pens, pencils, equipment, and supplies. They only take up space.

- Hang anything on the wall that you can—calendars, pictures, and wall shelves for reference books and directories. Use wall pockets for file folders.

Ten Tips for Reclaiming Your Desktop

Piles of clutter can be overwhelming, and can keep many people from even getting started on a job. Having a clean desk each day is very important to achieving productivity. It doesn't take long for your desk at home or at the office to become a catchall for things that really do not belong.

Once a desk gets out of control, you will need to take some time to get it back in order. Below are ten ideas to help you reclaim your desk.

- Have the necessary supplies you will need to get things ordered and under control such as a wastebasket, shredder, and file folders for paperwork you need to keep. Keep a separate waste container for paper you can recycle.

- Get rid of all loose business cards you really don't need. For business cards you want to keep, purchase a container to hold them for easy retrieval and accessibility.

- Toss all old catalogs. Hold current issues of catalogs in a sturdy organizer for easy retrieval.

- Recycle all magazines, newsletters, flyers, and coupons that are no longer current. Get into the habit of tossing all old magazines when the new issue arrives.

- Recycle junk mail. It's a complete waste of time (and paper!).

- Recycle loose notes, pieces of paper, and sticky notes with information that is unclear or outdated. If you use sticky notes, try using a file folder to house the notes. Label the file folder *Notes* and keep sticky notes inside. Keep the folder handy. All your notes will be in one place, easy to retrieve, and easy to recycle when you are finished.

- File as you go along. Keep a stack of file folders and felt markers. Make a new file folder for each category and file each piece of paper as you go along.

- Staple papers together that belong together. Avoid using paper clips.

- When filing, start with the paper on top and work from top to bottom.

- Keep a shredder handy so that when you come across sensitive paperwork that needs to be destroyed, you can take care of it immediately instead of stacking it into a new pile.

Increasing Productivity at Home and at Work

In these busy times, many women are asking, "How can I get more done in the time I have?" When given a certain amount of time to get a job done, I am amazed at the differences in how much one person can complete compared to someone else. The factors may include personality types, how rested a person is, and whether or not the job is enjoyable. But no matter how you perform there are some ways to increase productivity at home and on the job. The simple answer is to stop wasting time. Try one or more of the following suggestions:

- Similar tasks that must be done day in and day out— answering e-mails, placing calls, dropping children off at school and extracurricular activities—should be scheduled at the same time and place. This way you will already know what has to be done and when, well ahead of time. Schedule other activities and projects around those nonnegotiables.

- If you are working at a desk, make sure you are comfortable, the lighting is good, and you have all your tools nearby and handy. You don't want to be getting up and down looking for frequently used items. At home, you may want to have duplicates of much-used items in several locations, especially if you live in a two-story home.

- Are you a morning person or a night owl? Schedule your highest priority projects and work when you are at your most energetic.

- Pace yourself. You cannot work effectively at top speed all day long. Remember the tortoise and the hare? Slow and steady wins the race. Use those bursts of energy to finish at the end of the day or the end of a project.

- Focus on only one thing at a time, especially tasks that require your full concentration. Save multitasking for jobs that don't require too much brainpower.

- Take a break. Relax, stretch, and deep-breathe for a few minutes. Take a short walk if you can, or have a cup of tea or coffee so you are ready to get back to work full steam ahead!

How to Be Taken Seriously When Working from Home

This is a note for any of you who work part-time or full-time from home. Running a home-based business or working as a telecommuter can be difficult. The needs of family and life are still right there in front of you while you work. The laundry pile awaits. The dishes need to be done. Your office clutter grows by the minute. And one of the biggest obstacles to organizing your work life is managing time and interruptions. Family, friends, and neighbors might not respect your work time. You and others must take your work seriously so that you can be productive. Here are some tips to help you do just that:

- *Clearly define your work area.* Use a separate room, if possible. If an entire room is out of the question right now, use a partition, folding room divider, or other large piece of furniture in order to set aside your working area. It will help you, as well as everyone else, to see exactly where the home stops and your office space begins. If possible, close the door or partition while working so no one will have access.

- *Set definite boundaries in your working hours.* Let family and friends, as well as your customers, know precisely when you will be working. Post hours available for work and stick to them. If you respect your time, others will too.

- *Let others know when you do not wish to be disturbed.* Post a sign on the door or hang something from the door handle. Be firm but kind. After only a short time your family will know you need to be left alone.

- *Learn how to say no.* It is easy to become distracted by chores, invitations from friends, or pleas from your children. You need to find a balance, especially if you have children at home, keeping in mind that the reason you came home to work was because you wanted to have more time with your kids. But during scheduled working times, learn to say no to invitations that will keep you from completing work in a timely manner. You can certainly be flexible, but it is important to be consistent so people know they can depend on you.

- *Keep your work area as quiet as possible from outside noises.* You will be able to complete a great deal more if you don't become distracted by noise from the children playing, the television, the radio, or computer games.

- *Dress for success.* It is always important to look your best, especially if you work at home. You don't necessarily need to wear a dress, but casual working attire will go a long way toward letting everyone know you are serious and your business is important to you.

- *Keep your office organized and neat.* Nothing says "efficient" better than a tidy and organized office, especially your desk. It doesn't have to look pristine, but you will say "success" more quickly with a desk that has some sense of organization.

- *Have a separate phone or phone line for the business if possible.* This will help you maintain a much more professional image. An answering machine with children's voices or clever messages can be a real turnoff to potential clients. Make sure you use the answering machine during your off hours. Resist the temptation to answer the phone after regular business hours.

Working from home can be exciting and rewarding. Keeping the household and business boundaries definable will ensure success in your home-based business and will preserve your home and family time as sacred. It works to everyone's advantage!

Quick Tips for Working Efficiently

Whether you work from home or leave each morning to work away from your house, the same principles apply. We have a desire to work efficiently and productively, but interruptions, delays, and time-wasters often keep us from performing at our best. Try one or more of the following tips to help you keep focused and working.

Some of these ideas we have addressed in relation to other categories, but think of each of these in terms of how you work. The benefit of getting organized is that the healthy habits you acquire can be used in all parts of your life.

- Keep the items, files, and equipment that you use daily within reach. The items you use only once or twice a week can be close by but not in your working area. The things you use even less often can be stored elsewhere in the office or in another location to be retrieved when needed.

- Try not to have chairs near your desk. It is too easy for them to become clutter-keepers for stacks of papers, files, and books.

- If you work outside your home and have an office, try not to face your desk toward the door looking out. Each time someone passes by it becomes a distraction. It also encourages people to stop and chat.

- If you are busy on a project and suddenly remember something you need to do, don't stop and switch. Simply keep a scratch pad handy to jot a note to yourself.

- Try to give yourself a deadline for each project, even if it's self-imposed.

- Have an electronic timer at work to keep you on track. You will stay on task when you know the timer is ticking away.

Taking Charge of E-mail

- Don't answer e-mails every five minutes. Set aside time twice a day and set a timer for 15 to 30 minutes to answer and sort e-mail.

- Delete…delete…delete. Get rid of e-mails as quickly as you can. Inboxes fill up quickly.

- Be wary of attachments as they may contain harmful (and costly) computer viruses. Never open attachments from people you do not know.

- Set up e-mail folders. Transfer e-mails you wish to keep to the appropriate folder. This will help you keep the size of your inbox manageable.

- When sending e-mails DO NOT USE ALL CAPS! It's difficult to read and gives the impression that you're shouting.

- Put something in the subject line. It helps people find your e-mail more easily and is less likely to be inadvertently deleted.

- Use the KISS method. Keep it short and sweet.

- Unsubscribe from unnecessary lists. It's time-consuming.

- Respond to e-mail quickly.

- Reduce the time-waster e-mails like jokes, poems, and chain letters.

- Don't badmouth others, especially in e-mail. You don't know where it will go and once written down, it lasts forever!

- Don't forget to spell-check and proof!

Bringing Order to Your Online Life

Many of us love getting involved in social networks like Facebook and Twitter. That being said, there are some things about these networks that need to be discussed, especially among Christian women. Communication websites bring together people who have lost touch, help families stay connected when distance separates them, and give young, homebound moms a chance to reach out to their friends without having to leave their homes. Here are some ways to bring order to your online life.

- Always be polite. You really never know who is reading your information.

- Keep your private life private. If you feel the need to share something very personal with a friend, be discreet and give her a call. Once it is posted, it's hard to take it back.

- Be cautious who you add as a friend. Resist the urge to be a "friend collector." You need to choose your friends wisely.

- When asking for prayer be careful not to disclose information that is private. Social networks can become another means of gossip if not carefully watched.

- Don't talk about other people—you never know who their friends are. Remember—it's a small world!

- Don't give out too much information or personal information.

- Ask permission before you upload pictures of friends or their children. What is cute and adorable to you might be offensive to someone else. No matter how funny you think it is, your friend probably won't appreciate that photo of her choking on her punch being available to the entire Internet!

- Avoid too many applications. It can become wearisome to people to navigate through all the causes and games offered.

- Keep your messages simple, kind, and loving.

Make Your Computer Work for You

Computers have made life much faster and more efficient. That said, we need to utilize our computers to make them work for us—saving us time and making our jobs easier. This is true if you work out of the home, have an at-home business, or just enjoy creating on your computer. Below are some tips to make your computer work hard for you:

- Update your computer hardware at least every four to six years. You will be more productive if your computer is fast and efficient. But beware…don't be lured to upgrade too often. Sometimes adding extra space can gain you a few more years.

- Upgrade software when new features are added that you will be using for your job. You need to stay current.

- Name your files and folders with easy-to-remember categories and titles. You can't use it if you can't find it. You will waste too much time trying to remember the clever name you gave a file or folder.

- Back up your files daily or weekly. You only have to have one computer crash before this tip sinks in.

- When you are busy working on a document, remember to save your work often. I once lost 73 pages of typed work simply because I forgot to save. I learned quickly the importance of saving every few minutes.

- Learn your software. Buy an instruction book or take a class. The more features you know how to use, the more time you will save on a project.

- Add shortcuts to your desktop to get you to the program or application you need in a short amount of time.

- Always spell- and grammar-check your document!

- Preview your document before printing. You can eliminate paper and ink waste if you take a careful look at it before it goes to print.

Emilie's Essentials

The Multitasking File

One item that makes great use of space and effort is an accordion file. Go to your local stationery store and purchase one or a few. Accordion files are wonderful and oh, so versatile. You can use them to store bills for future payment, keep track of important papers, and gather greeting and thank-you cards for those special occasions.

Set the files up with labels. For example, your bills folder could have pockets labeled "Pay," "Read," "Answer," "Pending," and "Hold." Designate a shelf for a row of accordion files. You'll be able to store many of your most-needed paper items in these. And because accordion files are portable, you can take them with you to meetings so your records are handy or to the kitchen table when it's time to pay bills. Don't forget to purge them occasionally. The files won't serve you well if they are full of outdated or unneeded items.

Sheri's Secrets

Quick-Reference Organizer

A very good friend of mine gave me one of the best organizational ideas I have ever come across. Every time you visit a website to pay a bill, shop, or catch up with friends, you are required to provide a username and password. It can be tough to keep track of all the different names and passwords we have to enter!

On Lorrie's recommendation, I purchased a simple address book and stored all my online account information in it alphabetically. For example, if you go to abcstore.com, you can record your information under *A*. You can store your username, password, and other important information such as account numbers for bill paying. Make sure you keep this information in a safe place!

Chapter 7

Manage Your Money

Money-Saving Ideas for Families

Everywhere you turn you'll find new ideas for saving money. In the economic climate in which we find ourselves, we all would love to save money. The ideas below are simple suggestions that can save a little here and a little there. Before long, you'll have saved enough to make a dent in the family budget—or maybe enough to take a trip somewhere fun.

- Get your books from the library. It's hard to beat free.

- Review your telephone and cable bills for services you don't use and cancel them.

- Turn off the TV! Did you know that leaving the television on is the number-one electricity waster in the world? When everyone is finished watching television, especially before going to sleep, turn it off.

- Invite friends over instead of going out. Almost every activity at home is less expensive than going out. Host a cookout or a potluck meal, then play a game or have ice cream sundaes.

- Check to make sure none of the faucets in your household are leaking. A slowly dripping faucet can accumulate over two gallons per hour.

- Be kind to your freezer and refrigerator: Let hot food sit out for an hour (but no longer) before you put it in the fridge. Don't waste energy making your fridge work extra hard to cool it down.

- Turn off the lights in the rooms of your house that you are not occupying. Make it a habit to flip the switch each time you leave a room. Save electricity and save on your bill.

- Save your loose change, emptying it out of your purse and wallet once a week. Get the kids to help you roll it and deposit the money in the bank. It adds up fast!

- Get rid of unread magazine subscriptions. You should give their subscription department a call and try to cancel for a refund. Sometimes they'll give you the prorated amount back.

- Only run your dishwasher when full. Unless you have a newer dishwasher with a half-wash option, you use the same amount of water no matter how many dishes you put in.

- Fix broken appliances and repair torn clothing instead of throwing them away.

- If you skip the rinse and repeat instructions, you can cut your shampoo usage in half. This also goes for toothpaste, toilet paper, and dish soap. Just make it a habit to not use more than you need. A little moderation can really start to add up.

- Don't overspend on hygiene products. For most people, inexpensive hygiene products do the trick. The key is to use the basics regularly and consistently. You don't need to spend a lot to look and feel good.

- Exercise at home rather than joining a gym.

Savings on Your Automobile

A car can guzzle more than just gas. Maintenance, insurance, and upkeep can all take their toll on the wallet. Here are just a few suggestions that will save you money.

- Consider price comparisons for insurance. Recently I discovered that by adding my homeowners insurance policy to my car insurance company, I saved $350 dollars a year! Check out the competition. Everyone is looking for new customers, and you never know what deals or savings you might find.

- Don't fill up your gas tank at stations located near freeway or interstate exit ramps. They can be up to 20 cents higher.

- Check with your insurance company before purchasing a car. Different models can make a huge difference in the premium.

- If your keyless entry remote breaks you can save up to $50 by unscrewing and replacing the battery yourself rather than taking it to the dealer.

Keeping Your Utility Bills Down

Energy bills are never fun to pay. Although some factors (like extreme weather conditions) may be beyond your control, there are ways to make your use of energy more efficient and reduce your energy bills. Here are some tips and ideas to help stabilize those bills.

Heating

Your heating system is probably your home's biggest energy user in the winter. But it can quickly turn into an energy waster if you don't use it wisely.

- Leave the thermostat alone. During the day set it at

65 degrees or below, and at night turn it down to 55 degrees. You raise operating costs by five percent every time you raise the thermostat two degrees.

- Proper insulation keeps your home warm in winter and cool in summer. In fact, up to 20 percent of your heating energy can be lost through an uninsulated ceiling.

- Cut more heat loss by weather-stripping doors and windows. Close the damper when not using the fireplace or else heat will escape. Close off rooms not in use, along with heating vents, though not in more than 30 percent of the house. (Make sure you leave the vent nearest the thermostat open to ensure proper temperature sensing.) Turn off individual thermostats.

- Close draperies at night to keep out the cold. Open them during the day to let the sun shine through.

Lighting

Although individual lights don't use much energy, lighting costs can add up for a whole household. Here are some ideas on keeping lighting costs down.

- Fluorescent lights provide three times the light for the same amount of electricity as incandescent lights. They are very economical for bathrooms and kitchens, last ten times as long as incandescent bulbs, and produce less wasted heat.

- Dimmer switches can multiply bulb life up to 12 times while they reduce electricity use.

- Turn lights off when you're leaving a room and advise your family to do the same. Get in the habit of flicking off the switch!

- Let the light shine through. Lampshades lined in white

give the best light. Tall, narrow shades or short, dark-colored ones waste watts. (Dirt and dust absorb light too, so add bulb-dusting to your cleaning list.)

- One properly situated light in a room will do the work of three or four carelessly placed fixtures. Rearrange your room so the light is used more efficiently. If you're redecorating, use light colors. Dark colors absorb light.

- Don't use infrared heating lights for night lights or general lighting.

- Use lower-watt bulbs.

- Once you go to bed, turn off all outdoor lights except those necessary for safety and security.

Hot Water

Although hot water is the third-largest energy user in the average household, its use can be cut down painlessly.

- Consider flow-restricting devices. These devices can cut water consumption in half.

- Buy a water heater insulation blanket. This saves up to nine percent of your water heating costs.

- Fix the drips on all faucets. One drip a second can waste up to 700 gallons of hot water a year!

- Take showers instead of baths. The shower's the winner for less hot water use if you keep your shower time under five minutes. (If you need to wash your hair, do it in the sink. A shower just to shampoo is a hot water waster.)

- Monitor the use of the dishwasher. Run it once a day or less. It uses about 13 gallons each time instead of the 10 gallons each time you wash dishes by hand.

- Use cold water for the garbage disposal. It solidifies any grease and flushes it away easily.

- Turn down the temperature on your hot water heater to 140 degrees. (That's a "medium" setting if your dial isn't numbered.) If you don't have a dishwasher, 120 degrees may be adequate.

- When you go away on vacation, set the pilot setting on low or turn it off altogether. If you have an electric water heater, it may be the type on which the upper thermostat can be set 10 degrees lower than the bottom one.

How to Save Money at the Supermarket

Many busy families have surrendered to the fast-food phenomenon and very rarely cook at home. This is fine occasionally, but parents should be cautious of making it a routine. Those who find themselves on tight budgets will soon find the fast-food compromise more expensive than they anticipate. In many cases, it also deprives your family of balanced nutrition.

Don't view food preparation as drudgery, but delight in providing meals for your family. There are excellent cookbooks available that simplify food preparation. To ease your planning you might make up 3x5 cards giving you about seven different recipes for breakfast, lunch, and dinner. By rotating the cards, you can have variety and not get bored with your meals. Try to introduce a new recipe occasionally. If you have teenagers, they can be of great assistance. They can set the table, shop, clean vegetables, start the meal, serve the food, clean the table, and load the dishwasher. They can even help plan the menu! This is an excellent opportunity to teach your children many lessons for the adult life: meal planning, shopping for bargains, budget preparation, nutritional balance, table etiquette, time management in cooking meals, and meal cleanup.

We've listed several helpful hints below to help you at the supermarket. These should not only make the shopping experience more efficient, but also save you money. By putting even half of these ideas into action, you'll be surprised at how much time and money you'll save!

- *Shop with a purpose and a plan.* Plan your menus for the entire week (or two) and then organize your shopping list so that you have to pass through each section of the supermarket only once. Categorize your shopping list under headings like *Dairy, Meat, Produce, Freezer,* and *Grocery.* If you have to return to the first aisle to pick up just one thing, you may find yourself attracted by other items. This will push you over your food budget and cause you added stress.

- *Try to control your impulse buying.* Studies have estimated that almost 50 percent of purchases are entirely unplanned (that is, not on your list). Be especially careful at the start of your shopping trip when your cart is nearly empty. You're more susceptible to high-priced, unplanned purchases then.

- *Get your shopping done within a half hour.* This means you don't shop during rush hour. Shopping at busy times will hurry you up, and you will have a greater tendency to just pull items from the shelves without really shopping comparatively for the best product. Supermarkets are often very comfortable places to linger, but one study suggests that customers spend at least 75 cents a minute after a half hour in the store.

- *Shop alone if you can.* Children and even spouses can cause you to compromise from your list as they try to help you with unplanned purchases. Television advertising can cause great stress when your children go with you. They want to make sure they have the latest cereal, even though it is loaded with sugar and has very little nutritional value.

- *Never shop when hungry.* The psychology here is obvious. When you're hungry *everything* looks good, and you'll end up with food in your cart that you don't really need.

- *Use coupons wisely.* Food companies often use coupon offers to promote either new products or old products that haven't been selling well. Ask yourself if you would have bought the item had there been no coupon, and compare prices with competing brands to see if you're really saving money.

- *Be a smart shopper.* Be aware that grocery stores stock the highest-priced items at eye level. The lower-priced staples like flour, sugar, and salt are often below eye level, as are bulk quantities of many items. More and more specialty stores are carrying bulk food, which can give you excellent cost savings if you are buying for a large family or a picnic. When things are on sale, consider buying them in larger quantities. For example, a dozen cans of tuna can be stored indefinitely. Also, be aware that foods displayed at the end of an aisle may appear to be on sale, but often are not.

- *Check the unit pricing.* Purchase a small, inexpensive pocket calculator to take with you to the market. This way you can divide the price of the item by the number of units in the package to find the cost per unit. This way you can compare apples with apples. The lowest-priced container does not always have the cheapest price per unit.

- *Avoid foods that are packaged as individual servings.* Extra packaging usually boosts the price of the product. This becomes too expensive for families.

- *When buying meat consider the amount of lean meat in the cut as well as the price per pound.* A relatively high-priced cut with little or no waste may provide more meat for your money than a low-priced cut with a great deal of bone, gristle, or fat. Chicken, turkey, and fish are often good bargains for the budget buyer. And you'll gain extra savings by purchasing a whole chicken or turkey instead of butchered cuts.

- *Buy vegetables and fruits in season* since they'll be at their peak of quality and their lowest price. Green beans, in season, cost less per serving than canned beans and offer much more nutrition. Fresh produce also has better flavor and fewer additives. You might even want to consider planning an "old-time canning weekend." Canning produce yourself gives you the greatest economy and lets you enjoy these delicacies all throughout the year.

Tips for Buying in Bulk

At Costco and Sam's Club, there really is something for everyone! One friend refers to Costco as the "$200 Club" because he can't come out without having spent $200! Here are tips that will help you navigate the bulk-buying trend.

- Never shop when hungry. You will end up buying much more than you'd intended.

- Purchase only the products you use on a regular basis.

- Go with a list and stick to that list.

- Take the amount of cash you intend to spend. Leave your credit and debit cards at home. Once your money is gone, you're done. Take along a calculator to keep track of what you've spent.

- Compare the per-unit pricing for items you buy regularly. Sometimes the better deal may be at your local grocery store.

- Don't buy more than you have space to store when you get home, or more than your family can enjoy before the food spoils.

- Take along an ice chest or large cold bag to keep cold items at a safe temperature, especially in the summer or when you have other errands.

- Sample cautiously or you can get caught up in the moment and regret your purchase later.

- Consider finding a neighbor to share large purchases with to help with the cost and storage issues.

Here are some great nonperishable items that are handy to buy in bulk. Take the stress out of your life by keeping these items on hand!

- Paper products such as greeting cards, gift-wrapping paper, ribbon, boxes, mailing tape

- Extra school supplies

- Tape, glue, bulk office supplies

- Pet food

- Envelopes (legal and letter size)

- Paper plates and plastic silverware

- Special-occasion and party supplies, such as birthday candles, balloons, or decorative napkins

- Small gifts for friends, neighbors, and holiday drop-ins

- Postage stamps

- Shampoo and soap

- Toothpaste, toothbrushes, mouthwash

- Laundry and cleaning supplies

- Snacks for lunches

- Canned and bottled foods, condiments, and soft drinks

- Basic dry foods
- Blank CDs and DVDs
- Bestselling books and movies
- Camera accessories
- Various sizes of light bulbs
- Candles
- Small and large appliances and electronics

Saving Money with Weekly Menus

Planning a weekly menu is an essential skill for every woman. It will save a great deal of stress when five o'clock rolls around and you realize that, once again, you have no idea what to make for dinner! Maybe you decide on a dish but realize you're missing one or two key ingredients. So you run to the store to pick up the necessary items. You waste time on this last-minute errand—and tomorrow night you'll find yourself in the same position. In this case, a little planning goes a long way.

- On Saturday or Sunday, take 20 minutes to sit down with your cookbooks and recipes and plan meals— breakfast, lunch, and dinner—for the rest of the week.

- As you plan the meals, keep a running list of each meal's ingredients that you don't already have in the pantry. This will be the basis of your shopping list for the week.

- Be sure to add some healthy snack items to the list!

- If your menu includes fish or other items that spoil quickly, consider eating it early in the week or adding a brief midweek grocery store trip to ensure that your food is the freshest it can be. Don't let fish linger in the refrigerator for six days before it's cooked!

If you shop from this list and stick to your menu, you're

guaranteed to use all the food you buy. Nothing will go to waste, and you won't find forgotten vegetables rotting in the crisper!

Saving Money in the Laundry Room

Did you know that every load of laundry costs between $1.50 and $1.75? And the average family does between seven and ten loads of laundry per week! Here are some ideas that will help you save money while washing clothes.

- Switch to cold water for delicate blouses, skirts, and trousers. Cold water saves energy and money, and it's much gentler on delicate fabrics.

- Add half a cup of white vinegar to each load during the final rinse cycle and your clothes will smell fresher and hold their color longer. You also won't need to add a dryer sheet or fabric softener. This is especially useful for blankets, and helps to keep them soft and fluffy.

- Add half a cup of baking soda to the wash or rinse cycle to freshen your laundry. Clothes will be sweeter and cleaner smelling.

- To remove the water spots from fabrics, sponge the entire stained area with white vinegar and let stand a few minutes. Rinse with distilled water and let dry.

- To remove lipstick, liquid makeup, or mascara from fabrics, soak the clothing in dry-cleaning solution and let dry. Rinse and then wash.

- Do several loads of laundry back-to-back. As you dry one load after another, the dryer is already warm with the residual heat from the previous cycle. Your clothes will dry faster and save on energy used.

- Throw a new, clean tennis ball in the dryer. It will help the tumble dryer action and your clothes will dry faster.

- Set your dryer on auto. If you have this feature you will find it takes less time than you estimate to dry the clothes. And less dryer time saves on the life of your clothes and saves you money.

How to Teach Your Children About Money

We live in a world where adults often find themselves in financial woes. Where do we learn about money? Usually by trial and error, since few families take the time to teach their children how to be smart with money. Yet at an early age, children should know about money and what it can do for them. Children who learn about money at an early age will be ahead in this mystery game. Learning to deal with money properly will foster discipline, good work habits, and self-respect.

Start with an allowance.

Most experts advise that an allowance should not be tied directly to a child's daily chores. Children should help around the home not because they get paid for it but because they share responsibilities as members of a family. However, you might pay a child for doing *extra* jobs at home. This can develop his or her initiative. We know of parents who give stickers to their young children when they do something that they haven't specifically been asked to do. These stickers may then be redeemed for 25 cents each. This has been great for teaching not only initiative but also teamwork in the family.

An allowance is a vital tool for teaching children how to budget, save, and make their own decisions. Children learn from their mistakes when their own money has been lost or spent foolishly.

How large an allowance to give depends on your individual family status. It should be based on a fair budget that allows a reasonable amount for entertainment, snacks, lunch money, bus fare, and school supplies. Add some extra money to allow for church and savings. Be willing to hold your children responsible for living within their budget. Some weeks they may have to go without, particularly when they run out of money.

Model the proper use of credit.

In today's society we see the results of individuals and couples using poor judgment regarding credit. Explain to your children the conditions when it's necessary to use credit and the importance of paying back their loan on a timely basis. You can make this a great teaching tool. Give them practice in filling out credit forms. Their first loan might be from you to them for a special purchase. Go through all the mechanics that a bank would: Have them fill out a credit application and sign a paper with all the information stated. Teach them about interest, installment payments, balloon payments, and late payment costs. Teach them to pay on time responsibly.

Teach your children how to save.

At times we should deny our children certain material things so that they have a reason to save. As they get older they will want bicycles, stereos, a car, and a big trip. They need to learn the habit of saving so they can then buy these larger items.

One of the first ways to begin teaching the concept of saving is to give the children some form of piggy bank. Spare change or extra earnings can go into the piggy bank. When it gets full you might want to open an account at a local bank.

When your children are older you might want to establish a savings account at a local bank so they can go to the bank and personally deposit money to their account. This habit of depositing money will help your children begin thinking about saving.

In the end, children who learn how to save will better appreciate what they've worked to acquire.

Show them how to be wise in their spending.

Take your children with you when you shop, and show them some cost comparisons. They will soon see that with a little effort they can save a lot of money. You might want to demonstrate this principle to them in a tangible way when they want to purchase a larger item for themselves. Go with them to several stores to look for that one item, writing down the highest price and the lowest price for that item. This way they can really see how much they can save by comparison shopping.

Clothing is an area where a lot of lessons on wise spending can be made. After a while your children will realize that designer clothes cost a lot more just for that particular label or patch. Our daughter, Jenny, soon learned that outlet stores offered great bargains on well-made clothes. To this day she still likes to find excellent bargains by comparison shopping.

Let them work part-time.

There are many excellent part-time jobs waiting for your child. Fast-food outlets, markets, malls, and babysitting can give valuable work experience to your older children. Some entrepreneurial youngsters even begin a thriving business based on their skills and interest. Maybe they can do yard work for an elderly neighbor or take care of a friend's pets when the owners go on vacation. These part-time jobs are real confidence boosters. Just remember to help your child keep a proper balance between work, home, church, and school. A limit of 10 to 15 hours per week might be a good guideline.

Let them help you with your budgeting.

Encourage your children to help you budget for the family finances. This gives them experience in real-life money problems. They also get a better idea about your family's income and expenses. Children can have good suggestions about how to better utilize the family finances, and their experience can give them a better understanding of why your family can't afford certain luxuries.

Give them experience in handling adult expenses.

As your children get older they need to experience real-life costs.

Since children normally live at home, they don't always understand true-to-life expenses. Let them experience paying for their own telephone bill, car expenses, and clothing expenses. Depending upon the situation, having them pay a portion of the utility and household bills can be an invaluable experience for children who have left school and are still living at home.

In teaching children how to budget, one family gave each child several dollars a week. Each of these dollar bills was put into an envelope labeled *Church, Savings,* or *Fun.* Every week the church money was put in the collection plate, and once a month the savings money was deposited in the bank. The "fun" money was the child's to spend as he or she wished, but once it was gone it couldn't be supplemented from the other envelopes. The parents encouraged the children to spend the "fun" money on books, school supplies, and decorations for their bedrooms instead of cheap entertainment.

Show them how to give to the Lord.

At a very young stage in life, parents and children should talk about where things come from. The children should be aware that all things are given from God and that He is just letting us borrow them for a time. Children can understand that we are to return back to God what He has so abundantly given to us. This principle can be experienced through either Sunday school or their church offerings. When special projects at church come up, you might want to review these needs with your children so they can decide whether they want to give extra money above what they normally give to their church. Early training in this area provides a valuable basis for learning how to be a giver in life and not a taker.

Your children will learn about money from *you*, so be a good model. If you have good habits, they will reflect that; if you struggle with finances, so will they. One valuable lesson to teach them is that money doesn't reflect love. A hug, a smile, a kiss, or just time spent together is much more valuable than money.

Savings Everywhere

Saving money is on everyone's mind. Here are a few ideas to get the most out of what you purchase and save money on items you need.

- One week a month, declare a no-spend week. Other than essentials like groceries and gas, don't buy anything else during that week. No clothes, no DVDs, and no expensive lattes! Watch the savings add up.

- Instead of buying a new mattress, revive your old one by adding a piece of plywood on top of the box spring to re-firm it. And for real comfort, add a memory foam mattress topper.

- To get more out of your printer ink, ignore the warning light. Most printers have at least 20 percent of the ink left when the warning light comes on. Wait until you notice fading on your printed pages.

Seven Steps to Financial Cleanup at Tax Time

You can do a great financial cleanup yourself by breaking the job down into logical steps. Throwing everything out and making a clean start isn't the answer. Discarding salary stubs, last year's tax return, or current receipts for medical or business expenses will only bring you problems further down the road.

One of the biggest mistakes people make is not retaining records. Throwing away records that later turn out to be important cause people a lot of unnecessary work and worry. Well-kept financial records will pay off during emergencies. Should an accident occur, a friend or family member can quickly locate your insurance policy and the papers needed for vital information.

Here are seven steps to help you organize time and effort during tax-return time.

Know what to keep.

Keep permanent, lifetime records. These would include personal documents required for credit, job-qualification papers, Social Security and government program papers, birth and marriage certificates, Social Security number cards, property records, college credits, diplomas, and licenses. Also keep transitory records that pertain to your current circumstances: employee benefits, receipts for major purchases (auto, stock, jewelry, art), tax returns, insurance policies, credit union information, and canceled checks relating directly to home improvements. The IRS has the right to audit within three years. Let this be a measure of how long you keep receipts.

Set up your personal system according to your natural organization.

If you are disorganized, your system should be simple. Keep it uncomplicated. The less time you have, the simpler your system should be. If you like working with numbers and are good in math, your system can be more complex.

Set aside a spot for your records.

Obtain a safe deposit box for permanent documents plus a fireproof and waterproof filing cabinet for home use.

Let someone know where your records are kept.

Make a list of the location of your insurance policies and give it to a family member, a trusted friend, or even your pastor.

Get professional advice when you need it.

Expert advice can go a long way and, in the long run, save you time and money. Accountants are a great source of information and many times save much more than their cost. Financial planners are helpful if your past history has been a financial disaster, and they can help you avoid future mistakes.

Review your will and insurance policies annually.

What worked last year may need some revisions this year. Make sure your family understands your final goals.

Record-keeping requires time set aside.

You must discipline yourself to set aside a time each month to go over your financial records so you won't be overwhelmed in April when you have to file your tax return. Some people update weekly when paying bills or when reconciling checking accounts.

Great record-keeping gives mental benefits as well as more hours to do things you enjoy doing. God will honor and bless you as you keep order in your financial life.

Ten Things to Do Instead of Spending Money

In a time of economic recession, most people are watching their pennies. Experts say many times we go shopping simply because we are bored. Bringing order to our temptations will save our money and sanity. So when the urge strikes to hop in the car and visit the store, try one or more of these ideas instead.

- Wash all your hairbrushes and combs. Plug the bathroom sink and fill it with hot water and a tablespoon of shampoo. Soak your brushes in the water for thirty minutes. If you have a brush without any fabric, use an old toothbrush to scrub it clean. Clean out excess hair and rinse the brushes with hot water. Let dry.

- Clean out the silverware drawer.

- Clean out one shelf in your linen closet.

- Go through your bathroom cabinets and throw out all your old makeup, nearly empty bottles of lotions, and expired medicines.

- Gather all your old magazines and newspapers and put them inside one of your reusable grocery bags. Take them to the recycling bin.

- Clean the pet dishes with soap and water, then run them through the dishwasher to sanitize.

- Call an old friend you haven't talked to in a while.
- Write a note of thanks or encouragement to a staff member at your church.
- Try a new recipe and serve it for dinner.
- Pick some flowers from your garden for the dinner table. Light a candle and enjoy your family!

Do you see how easy it can be to stop wasting money and start investing in your life in simple ways? Think of your own ideas to add to this list. And the next time your kids want to wander around the shopping mall, ask them to think of their own list of things to do that are free, helpful, and creative. You might just start a new habit that saves you many days of boredom and enriches your life tenfold.

Emilie's Essentials

Wisdom for Life

Let's hear it for simple, straightforward ideas! Scripture is filled with wisdom, advice, and guidelines for understanding and managing money and resources.

- The rich rules over the poor, and the borrower is servant to the lender.—Proverbs 22:7
- If anyone does not provide for his own, and especially for those of his household, he has denied the faith and is worse than an unbeliever.—1 Timothy 5:8
- How much better is wisdom than gold, and understanding than silver!—Proverbs 16:16 TLB
- Whoever gathers money little by little makes it grow.—Proverbs 13:11 NIV
- Much is required from those to whom much is given, for their responsibility is greater.—Luke 12:48 TLB

Chapter 8

Bring Peace to Daily Life

Infuse a Day with Cheer

Here are a few simple ideas to cheer you on—and up!

- If you want some creative time to yourself—schedule it!
- Plan an afternoon to write, paint, dream.
- Surprise your family some evening and eat dinner in the living room. Or when it warms up, set up a card table in the backyard for a special candlelit meal.
- A little extra touch here and there can make a lot of difference—even if it's only to you. A ribbon around the dinner napkins or a single flower in a vase on the entry table or a sachet in a bowl by the bathroom sink—all these things can breathe new life into a room.
- Here's a bonus tip: Take advantage of a free hour to write a love note to your husband or to your children.

Add a Touch of Hope

Your home and life will have more peace and order when you add a touch of hopefulness to your environment. For starters, take a cup of tea and wander through the room where you spend the majority of your time. Whether it is an office, a family room, or your kitchen, examine the colors and the arrangement of furniture. What is there about the room that makes you feel energized, ready to move forward? Pictures of your family? A memento from a special trip? Light coming through the window? Music in the background? Lit candles, or flowers sitting on your table?

Simple as it sounds, all of these things can build a more hopeful atmosphere. When you are encouraged by the hope that comes with trusting God, your home will show it. Don't just save such a feeling for guests who come through your doors, but shower yourself and your family with the joy of a cozy, luminous household. Delight in the treasures of your heart and your hope that are reflected in your home.

Getting the Most out of Telephone Time

One of our favorite inventions of all time is the telephone. It can also become a huge time-waster. How can you be more productive on the telephone?

- Make sure you have enough telephones in your home located in strategic spots and rooms.

- If the telephone is located on your desk, place it on your left if you are right-handed and on the right side if you are left-handed. Then you can talk and write at the same time.

- Hang it on the wall if space is at a premium.

- When leaving a message speak up clearly. Repeat your telephone number slowly at the beginning of the message and again at the end.

- Place a time limit on your calls. Set a timer if you need to. Let the caller know immediately if you only have a few minutes to spare.

- Get to your point or bring the other person to their point.

- Take care of the business at hand first, then if time allows, you can spend a few minutes socializing.

- When leaving a message let the person know the best time to call you back.

- Have a clock visible if a timer is unavailable. It's amazing how quickly time passes while on the phone.

- Screen your calls when involved in something important. You don't need to pick up the phone every time it rings—that's why you have caller ID and voice mail!

- Don't feel guilty about hanging up on unsolicited sales calls. Be firm but polite when you tell the caller that you're not interested.

- Be prepared with everything you need before you make your call.

How to Organize Your Handbag

Remember the last time you rummaged through your handbag digging through old receipts, papers, wads of tissue, half-used lipsticks, unwrapped Lifesavers, and that unmailed letter you thought was lost months ago? Handbags have a way of becoming catchalls, places where you keep everything and can't find anything. You can get your handbag into top shape with just a little effort and organization. If you keep a well-organized handbag, it will be simple to change bags and do it quickly.

Gather together a nice-sized handbag for everyday and three to seven small purses in various colors and sizes. (The small purses can be of quilted fabric, denim, or corduroy prints with zipper or Velcro fasteners.) Organize these purses as follows:

- Wallet
  - Money/checkbook
  - Change compartment
  - Pen
  - Credit cards
  - Pictures

- Driver's license
- Calendar (current)

- Makeup Bag 1
  - Lipstick
  - Comb/small brush
  - Blush
  - Mirror

- Makeup Bag 2
  - Nail file
  - Small perfume
  - Hand cream
  - Nail clippers
  - Scissors (small)
  - Tissues
  - Breath mints/gum/cough drops
  - Matches

- Eyeglass Case
  - For sunglasses

- Eyeglass Case
  - For reading/spare glasses

- Small Bag 1
  - Business cards—yours and your husband's, hair-dresser, insurance agent, auto club, doctor, and dentist
  - Library card
  - Seldom-used credit cards

- Small calculator
- Aspirin
- Small Bag 2
  - Reading material—small Bible, paperback book
  - Cleanup wipes
  - Needle/thread/pins/thimble
  - Band-Aids
  - Toothpicks
  - Feminine protection

By taking some time to set it up, you can organize your purse and avoid last-minute frustration and stress. You'll never be digging for nail clippers again—you know they're right in your second makeup bag!

Planning for the Unexpected

When traveling out of the home with small babies and young toddlers, it's best to plan for the unexpected. If we've learned anything raising kids, it's that if something *can* happen, it will! So many families (especially moms) spend a great deal of time in the car. It only makes sense to keep an emergency bag or box with items you might find yourself in need of when the unexpected happens. Use a diaper bag, plastic shoe box, or a reusable grocery store bag to store some or all of the following:

- A change of clothes; pajamas
- An extra pair of shoes and socks
- A roll of paper towels
- Three diapers (and a couple of plastic grocery bags for dirty diapers)
- Flushable wet wipes

- Band-Aids and antiseptic wipes
- Crackers and juice box snacks (to use in case of an unexpected long wait)
- Small coloring book and crayons
- Bib, cup and/or bottle
- Baby Tylenol
- Pacifiers
- Extra blanket
- A few toys

Check for refilling every three to four months. Keep these items stored in the trunk so you will be prepared for the unexpected twists and turns of motherhood.

Unfinished Business

Do you ever feel like you're running in circles? Do you put off new pursuits because you are spending your precious time juggling projects that are never completed? Make a list of five projects you would love to finish and tackle these one at a time. You'll find that as you clear away the unfinished business, you'll be free to reach for new pursuits. Don't delay your goals and aspirations.

Which terminal projects are eating up the most time? Give yourself an absolute deadline to complete each one or consider letting go of the project altogether. Which projects are the most overwhelming and which have the highest priority? If you take care of a couple that are time sensitive, you'll give yourself breathing room and a sense of accomplishment. Consider the ones that absolutely must get done because others are counting on them or because they have a deadline. There's your starting place!

The 80/20 Rule

The 80/20 rule is one of the greatest principles you can use to figure out your top priorities. If all of the items on your to-do list are arranged in order of value, 80 percent of the value comes from only 20 percent of the items. The remaining 20 percent of the value comes from 80 percent of the items.

The 80/20 rule suggests that in a list of ten projects, finishing two of them will yield 80 percent of the value. So don't be overwhelmed by a large list. What's left undone today can go on the list for tomorrow. Rearrange your to-do list in order of priority and keep the 80/20 rule in mind.

Choose Contentment

When you're overwhelmed, you can't see new opportunities or face daily challenges. It can be a struggle to even care for your family! "Are you kidding?" you say. "I've got too much to handle already!" If you want to eliminate mess and clutter from your life, ask yourself these questions: Who am I? Where am I going? What do I need to do to get there? Does this improve the quality of my life? You can choose to be content. But as long as you choose discontent, you'll have clutter in your personal affairs. These basics are lifetime pursuits in growing into the woman that God wants you to become.

Don't Delay Small Tasks

Do small chores as needed so they occupy the least amount of time possible. Put a shirt back on the hanger, repair the sag on the rear gate, replace that burned-out lightbulb, and put new batteries in your smoke alarm. If you start taking care of the immediate tasks rather than saving them for later, you'll notice an amazing difference in your clutter problem. The small stuff adds up to big projects later—don't let them snowball.

As you go about your day today, pay attention to which tasks can be done immediately. The dishwasher can be loaded, the cereal box can be put in the cupboard, the dining room table can be cleared so that it's clean for dinner, and your paid bills can be filed. Things are looking better already!

Do You Have Enough Space?

Do you have sufficient space for your stuff? If so, is your space effective? There is a difference. You may have too much stuff for your space. If that is the case, you will have to make some tough decisions about what will make the cut and what has to go.

Make sure you have adequate storage containers that work best in your space. Maybe cardboard or plastic storage boxes work best for you, or maybe you like to use cubes and decorative baskets. Don't forget to try "space bags" for seasonal clothing, blankets, quilts, and other bulky items.

Begin using the 15-minute method and work through your closets and drawers to de-clutter and restructure your living space. The choices are simple: Store it properly or get rid of it.

Big Ideas, Small Spaces

If you're running out of space—keep reading! I have a friend who lives in a small beach apartment—and believe me, there's absolutely no wasted space. She's installed a towel rack on the inside of a closet door to hang tablecloths. Her armoire stores her DVDs, CD player, and radio. And on the top she keeps her decorative baskets.

Boxes are great storage places. Cover them in bright colors to match your rooms and store away! You can use the top of everything—refrigerator, cabinets, hutches. Just make sure it looks neat and decorative and you've got great storage areas. And you know that luggage you have sitting around? Fill them right up with items you need to store, like your out-of-season clothing or your collection of summer sandals!

Vertical Storage

Vertical storage is one of the most overlooked ways to maximize your space. Look for slim, tall bookcases to store more than just books. In a child's room a bookcase can hold toys, books, awards, and pictures.

Don't forget to hang anything you can. The whole room will look neater and less cluttered when items are off the floor. Decorative hooks can hold purses, coats, and hats. You can hang pots and pans in the kitchen. Shelves placed in a child's room can hold toys, stuffed animals, and other collectibles. Shelves in other areas can hold a teacup collection or pretty vases. Stereo speakers can often be hung high on the wall to free up more space on the floor or cabinet.

If you have the space, you should also consider installing a shelf that runs above the rod in your closet. This is a great place to store little-worn shoes, sweaters, and out-of-season clothing. In your closet, make use of closet organizers to store bulky sweaters, sweatshirts, and jeans. You'll be amazed at how much space this frees up! You can also put hooks over the bedroom or closet door to hang nightgowns and bathrobes. Get creative and make good use of all that free space!

Get a Cleaning Buddy

A clutter buddy is someone with whom you can trade de-cluttering time. A cleaning buddy has many advantages. She'll give you the motivation to get going and the accountability to *keep* going! Make sure you both have at least one day each week where you can devote at least one hour of time. Take turns going to each other's home. This person should be able to be objective about your "stuff." Spend some time getting ready to work by setting boundaries, such as not throwing out something without permission.

Choose which cabinet, drawer, or closet you will be working on ahead of time. Make sure you have the appropriate tools (trash bags, storage boxes, etc.) so that as you make decisions you can take care of storing, giving away, or getting rid of the clutter. As you get to work, set a timer and move quickly.

And don't forget to reward yourselves when you are finished with a small treat or lunch out together!

Keeping a Clutter-Free Zone

Once you have gone through an area in your home and organized it, declare it a clutter-free zone. No one is allowed to put anything there that doesn't belong—at any time, for any reason! The extra space you have acquired by getting rid of something should not be replaced with something else. Open space is an instant stress-reducer. Hit this idea home until it becomes a way of keeping your home tidy!

Let's Get Practical

Shall we get really practical? Here are some handy tips for practical organization around the house.

- If you're anything like me, you may be a bit challenged when it comes to electrical things. If so, color-code your extension cords when you have several at one outlet.

- Sew extra buttons for your clothing on the inside or at the bottom of an item. No looking around for just the right button when you need it!

- Tape the extra screws that come with furniture to the underside of chairs, sofas, and tables.

- Always refill that gas tank *before* it's on empty!

- Take inventory of your pantry or primary kitchen food cupboards and see what items seem to never get used and which ones are always being restocked. Keep this information on a list so that you can streamline your next trip to the grocery store.

When Order Gets in the Way

Luke 10 tells the story about two sisters: Mary and Martha. Martha becomes upset because she has done so much work to prepare for Jesus's visit while Mary has neglected the chores to spend time with their guest. Jesus tells Martha, "Mary has chosen that good part, which will not be taken away from her" (verse 42). I so want to be like Mary—but Martha gets in the way. She wants to cook and clean and have everything in order before her guests arrive. I'm sure Martha mopped and cleaned all day before Jesus arrived. But Mary understood that spending time with Jesus was more important, and that the preparation needed to take place in her *heart*. Our prayer is that you will have a passion for Jesus, and that we will all learn to say no to good things to make room for the very best things in our lives and the lives of our family members, friends, and neighbors. Don't settle for hurried activities when there is a chance for meaningful matters to emerge. Is your daughter crying over a skinned knee when there's laundry to be folded? Is your son at the point of tears over a difficult homework assignment just as you need to get dinner on the table? Does your husband need to discuss his day when the dog has made a mess in the entryway? Consider the Mary and Martha principle as you decide which situation takes priority!

Is There Compromise in Organization?

When cleaning and organizing your home there is a time and place for compromise—especially with your spouse. There's even room for compromise when dealing with your children and their accumulation of "stuff."

Find out what is most important to your husband in the area of order and cleanliness. If he wants the front room picked up when he comes home so that he can relax and unwind, you can compromise in that area and make cleaning the front room a priority every day. But make sure he understands that once you have picked it up, he must keep it picked up.

If everyone in the family takes their shoes off as soon as they walk in the door, find a nice large basket and have everyone dump their shoes there...but only there. Take control and insist that there can no longer be piles of shoes everywhere else.

Almost every child likes to accumulate "stuff," and children's rooms can often get out of control. As you're teaching your children to clean their rooms, be firm in the amount of storage they can have. If they don't have room for all their stuffed animals, clothes, or toys, some of them will have to go. Don't try to make this choice for your child, though. Leave that responsibility up to him.

Pick your battles and remember that communication and consistency are important keys to keeping harmony in the home when it comes to organization.

Car Container

That car of yours has a gem of a storage space! What, haven't you noticed? It's your *glove compartment.* Are you shocked? Who ever heard of organizing the glove compartment? Laugh if you will—but believe me, having the items on this checklist on hand will help in all kinds of stressful situations.

- State and local maps
- Car manual
- Notepad and pen
- Tire-pressure gauge
- $20 for emergencies
- Cleanup wipes
- Sunglasses
- Plastic forks and spoons
- Change for parking
- Business cards
- Band-Aids
- Note cards
- Scissors
- Nail clippers

The Idea Jar

If you can't decide what to do next to make your home better organized, try this. Cut some paper into strips and write down the various projects that need to be done on each of those strips. Place them in a jar and mix them up. When you need to decide what comes next, go to the jar and select one slip of paper. If it reads, "declutter the pantry," that's what you do next. When you need another task, go back to the jar and reach in. Bam! You have your next project! As new projects come to mind, write them down on slips of paper and drop them in the jar.

The idea jar is great for kids too! Create one that has age-appropriate projects for your children. When it is chore day or the kids are grumbling because there is nothing to do, bring out the jar.

Facebook Etiquette

If you have not joined the Facebook craze, watch out, you may find yourself becoming part of the more than 500 million users! Facebook is the new wave of communication for women and men, especially those with young children, or families that are separated by miles. It is relatively easy to use and provides information that can be shared with all your "friends." You can also locate friends you have lost touch with. You can update followers on what you're reading, movies you enjoyed, and even share pictures and prayer requests!

But just like any other form of technology, you need to be wise in how you use Facebook. Here are some guidelines to keep in mind for those who can't resist logging on and chatting with their friends.

- Set a definite time limit for yourself. Use a timer and decide ahead of time how long you can afford to spend at the computer. And then stick to the time you have allowed for yourself. It's very easy to lose track of time as you catch up with friends on social networks!

- Be careful what information and pictures you upload on your Facebook page. Once it is posted it is there forever!

- Keep your privacy setting on "Only Friends." You never know who could be trying to view your personal information! These privacy settings allow you to keep better control of the information you post.

- Ask permission before you publish pictures of your friends or children's pictures. You need to exercise extreme caution so as not to put someone in harm's way.

- Choose your words carefully. Since there are no voice inflections or facial expressions on the computer, your words may come across differently than you intended. Remember, kindness should always be the rule.

- Never, never lash out in anger to someone on your Facebook page. Those words can travel further than you could ever imagine, and they can never be taken back.

- If you are planning an event or an outing, send personal messages or set up an event in order to invite people privately. Only post invitations to a gathering publicly if you intend it to be an open house. Otherwise, feelings can get hurt and people can feel left out of the group. Try to be inclusive rather than exclusive.

- Remember, be careful but have lots of fun making new friends and keeping in touch with those you love.

Simple Ways to Help the Environment

We live in a time when being conscious of our environment is very important. Here are some simple ideas for changes in your home that really can make a difference. Get the family on board and see what a difference you can make in your corner of the world.

- Make it a habit to purchase products that are biodegradable.

- Separate your recyclables. Teach your children this habit.

- Fix leaky faucets and toilets. A small leak adds up quickly. A leaky faucet can waste 3,000 gallons of water a year.

- Use cloth diapers for your children that can be reused many times. Use disposable diapers only while traveling.

- Recycle bottles and cans. Not only does recycling clean up the waste, but it can also be a great way to earn extra money and save at the grocery store!

- Drive less. Walk whenever possible. Carpool if you can. More than a third of all private vehicle mileage is due to travel for work. Carpooling saves gas and cuts down on pollution, as well as greatly decreasing your automobile expenses.

- Dress appropriately for the weather. You can reduce your heating and air conditioning costs just by wearing the right clothing indoors.

- Take a shower instead of a bath. You'll use half the water.

- Recharge those batteries! With more and more toys and equipment using batteries as a power source, buy rechargeable ones rather than disposables.

- Clean your dryer screens. A clogged screen makes the dryer work harder, using as much as 20 percent more energy to dry one load of laundry. Clean it out before you dry every load.

- Plant a tree. You don't need to wait for a special occasion to do this with your family!

- Wash your car from a bucket. Fill a ten-gallon bucket with warm water and auto wash detergent. Use a soft terrycloth to wash the car, and only use the hose for rinsing. This technique can save between 100 and 150 gallons of water!

- Pick up litter, even if it's not your own.

- Try composting. It's amazing how many pounds of compost a family can generate in a year! Your plants will love the nutrients you add to the soil, and the compost also reduces the amount of water needed for each plant.

- Reuse computer paper. Turn it over and use the backside for printing. Or take a stack of sheets that have writing on one side, cut them into fourths, staple the sheets together, and create a no-cost notepad.

- If everyone in America would buy just one package of 100 percent recycled paper napkins instead of their regular brand, we would save a million trees a year! Cloth napkins are also a way to dress up your table and save costs at the same time!

- Try purchasing locally grown food, especially fruits and vegetables. When you buy locally, you help conserve fuel and reduce pollution. The benefit? Delicious, fresh food.

- Store canvas bags in your trunk so they'll always be ready when you go to the grocery store. We use approximately 100 billion plastic bags a year, and reusable canvas bags cut down on waste substantially.

- When you shop and purchase a large item or just one or two small items, forget the bag. Just place the item in your purse or carry it.

I believe we can learn to reuse and recycle without making ourselves crazy. Try one or two of these ideas to help take care of the beautiful world God has given us. You don't need to implement all these ideas at once, just try a new one each week. Why not make conservation a family project? Make a list of your favorite ideas and get started!

Organizing Your Prayer Time

During the early years of motherhood, it's often easy to become frustrated about your personal prayer time. You want to spend quality time with the Lord, but because of your busy schedule it just never works out in a practical way.

It's our hope that we can help you get back on track and become more thoughtful and deliberate about your time with the Lord. This method has transformed our prayer lives, and it's our earnest prayer that it will transform yours as well!

First, purchase an inexpensive binder, one package of divider tabs, and one package of lined paper. Label the tabs with the days of the week. Next, make a list of all things you want to pray for—family, finances, church, missionaries, etc. Finally, delegate these requests into your prayer notebook behind each tab. For example, on Mondays you might pray for each member of the family. On Tuesdays pray for your church, pastor, staff, and their work in the community and in the world. On Wednesdays pray for people who are ill and suffering, and so on. The Sunday tab is for sermon notes and outlines. Filter any prayer requests into the weekly tabs so your prayer time does not overwhelm you. Begin by spending some time reading the Bible, then open your prayer notebook to the tab for that day and pray for the items behind that tab. Do the same the next day, moving on through the rest of the week.

You might also want to create a prayer basket. Find a medium-sized decorative basket and fill it with a Bible, your prayer notebook, a few postcards, a box of tissues, and a small bunch of silk flowers. Place your basket in an area you pass daily, perhaps on a table, the kitchen counter, your desk, or even in the bathroom.

Schedule a daily time to spend time with your prayer basket in the morning, afternoon, or evening. Plan this time to pick up your basket and take it to a quiet place where you will use the basket's contents during your prayer time.

Write a short note to someone who needs encouragement on your postcards. Or you might simply say, "I prayed for you today." Some days you might cry through your whole prayer time. If so, the tissue is right there in your basket. The flowers give encouragement and lighten your heart as you look at God's creation.

A prayer basket is so personal and special. It's a daily reminder to spend time with God and seek His direction for that day. Proverbs 16:3 says, "Commit your works to the LORD and your plans will be established" (NASB).

On the days you pick up your prayer basket, your day, life, and organization as a busy woman will run so much more smoothly. Ask God for the strength to meet the demands of your schedule and deal with all the stress and challenges you may face. Trust Him to answer!

Emilie's Essentials

Divide Big Jobs into Fast Tasks

I recommend you not look at the big tasks ahead of you. You will become overwhelmed and easily discouraged. It is better to learn how to break the whole into smaller parts which become "fast tasks." These are little jobs you can readily handle. And step-by-step, you'll get the job done. Any of your tasks can be broken into small parts. The whole doesn't have to be accomplished in one sitting. Some might take you several days.

A good example might be when you want to reorganize the refrigerator. Set a time and work for 15 minutes. Work as fast as you can and get as much done as you can in that allotted time. If you didn't finish all you wanted to, tomorrow is another day and another 15 minutes. The same is true for cleaning out a cupboard or cleaning out the hall closet. Putting in a little bit of effort each day is better than not even attempting the project because it looks too big. You can always manage the fast tasks when you are over-whelmed with the whole.

Sheri's Secrets

A Legacy of Love

As I grow older I am finding myself less attached to some of my "treasures"—items that not too many years ago I would have been devastated to lose. As I set my sights on heavenly treasures that will not collect dust, I find I am working toward loosening my death grip on some of my "stuff." All my life I have been defined by the things I have accumulated over the years—things with which I was sure I could never part.

I have a dear friend of my heart, Wilma, who is creating a legacy of love with some of her possessions. Recently, she decided that it had become too much work to decorate for Christmas as she had always done so beautifully over the years. So near the holiday she hosted a special giveaway party for some of her treasures. She displayed her decorations and laid them out around her home for her family and special friends to look at, take home, and enjoy. She gave her treasures to us while she was still able to watch us enjoy them.

Wilma has also been gifting me for several years with beautiful crystal and tea dishes because I entertain often and she knows I will use them. She gets to enjoy their beauty and she doesn't have to wash and store them!

Maybe this is an idea you can begin thinking about for your own family and friends, or maybe for a young couple just starting out who can benefit from the "overflow" of items you no longer need or use. Blessing others with our gifts can be a great way of honoring what God has so graciously given to us.

"Do not lay up for yourselves treasures on earth, where moth and rust destroy and where thieves break in and steal; but lay up for yourselves treasures in heaven, where neither moth nor rust destroys and where thieves do not break in and steal. For where your treasure is, there your heart will be also."—Matthew 6:19-21

Chapter 9

Preparing for and Enjoying the Seasons

New Year Organization

After finishing a seminar on how to organize your household, I talked to a young mother who said, "I loved all the organizational ideas and tips you gave for the family and the home, but what about me—my personal organization?" Organization really does begin with our own personal lives. Once we have ourselves organized, we can move into the other areas of our lives such as our home or job.

Here are the tools you need to make your own daily planner.

- A small purse-sized binder with paper
- Dividers with blank tabs you can label yourself
- A calendar

Label your tabs as follows:

Tab 1: Goals

List long-term and short-term goals including daily, weekly, monthly, and yearly priorities. This will help you get your priorities in order. Include the following: Scriptures to read, prayer requests, and family, spiritual, household, personal, work-related, financial, and budget goals.

Tab 2: Calendar

Purchase a small month-at-a-glance calendar at a stationery store and insert it into your binder. As you learn to write activities and commitments down, you will be surprised at how much less complicated your life becomes.

Tab 3: Daily Planner

In this section, list your daily appointments from morning to evening. This is not only useful for the mother who works outside her home but also for the homemaker who wants to get her daily household duties done in a more orderly manner.

Tab 4: To Do, To Buy

Make a note here of all the things you need to do when you have an errand day, such as:

- Pick up winter coat at the cleaners.
- Go to the grocery store for birthday candles.
- Take package to the post office.
- Buy vitamins at health food store.

Tab 5: Notes

Here is a place to write down notes from:

- Speakers and sermons
- Meetings and Bible studies
- Projects

Tab 6: Miscellaneous

Keep topical lists in this section such as:

- Emergency phone numbers
- Dentist/physician phone numbers

- Babysitters' phone numbers
- Favorite restaurant phone numbers
- Books and music recommended

Tab 7: Expense Account

This section is especially for work-related expense outside the home.

- The date
- The amount spent
- What the expense was for
- Who purchased the item
- How it was paid for (cash, check, debit, credit)

Tab 8: Prayer Requests

Often when we're out to coffee with friends, or just chatting with a coworker, we'll hear about someone in trouble and say "I'll be praying for her." But do we always remember? Next time this comes up, take a few seconds to jot the request down in this section.

Some people like to date the request when they enter it into the organizer and then record the date when it is answered. If you do this, over a period of time you will have a history of how God has worked in your life. Remember, too, that not all prayers are immediately answered by a firm yes or no. Some are put on hold for a while.

I'll guarantee that by implementing these few helpful ideas into your new year, you'll be well on your way to the organized you.

The Decorator Notebook

The next time you see a decorating idea on a television show or in a magazine, cut out a picture or take notes and put the information in a "Decorator Notebook" you create. The notebook can be a three-ring binder with dividers (one for each room), a blank journal or sketch book from your local bookstore, or any other notebook you might have available. Keep it handy so you can access and add to it easily.

The next time you are out shopping, grab your notebook and take it along. You never know when you might find a great deal on a piece of furniture or accessory that might fit what you are trying to create.

Your notebook can also hold swatches of material, paint chips for the current color of a room, or a color or material sample of what you might like to add to a room to redecorate. The more organized you are in planning for organization and decorating, the greater chance you have of getting started and completing a project in a timely manner.

Spring Cleaning

As winter begins to melt away, we get excited and motivated to get our homes in order. It's time to throw open the windows and let in the spring air! But it takes a bit of organization and a few tips in order to get started. Just remember, it can take less time than you think. Jobs that you anticipate taking two hours might actually take just a few minutes.

So let's get started with these three thoughts in mind: *Do it! Do it right! Do it right now!*

Cleaning Products to Have on Hand

- All-purpose cleaner
- Floor products (waxes plus cleaners for vinyl or wood floors)
- Bathroom products (disinfectant, tile cleaner, mildew remover)
- Furniture polish
- Cleaning pads
- Scouring powders

- Metal polish
- Silver polish
- Window cleaner
- Dishwashing detergent or powder
- Rug and carpet cleaners
- Upholstery cleaners (Scotchgard after cleaning to protect against staining)
- Bleach, liquid or dry
- Fabric softener, liquid or sheets
- Prewash stain removers
- Oven cleaner (be sure to use rubber gloves with this type of cleaner)
- Drain cleaner
- Toilet bowl cleaner (a pumice stone is a must for removing the ring around the bowl)
- General cleaners (vinegar, ammonia, baking soda)

Cleaning Tools to Have on Hand

- Rubber gloves
- Vacuum cleaner, plus attachments for those hard-to-reach places (blinds, baseboards, radiators, shutters, corners in furniture, mattresses, ceilings, and walls)
- Dust cloth
- Feather duster
- Brushes for corners, tile, grill, etc.
- Paper towels
- Bucket
- Rags

- Broom and dustpan
- Stepladder or stepstool
- Mop
- Floor polisher or shampoo rug cleaner (optional)

Methods to Try

- Do one room at a time. Don't hurry; be thorough.
- Make a chart and delegate some of the jobs to the family.
- Each week reward your family by making their favorite pie, cake, or dinner.
- Take short breaks and eat an apple or have a cup of tea. You want to keep up your energy, not wear yourself out!
- Take cleaners with you from job to job and room to room by putting them in a bucket, a plastic carryall, or a basket.
- Turn on the radio for music to work by. Make it lively music so you can work faster.
- Time yourself by setting a timer. It's amazing what you can accomplish in 15 minutes.
- Upholstery furniture pieces can be brushed and vacuumed clean. This removes surface dirt and should be done four times a year.
- To remove dark or burned stains from an electric iron, rub the stain with equal amounts of white or cider vinegar and salt, heated first in a small aluminum pan. Polish in the same way you do silver.
- If your carpet has an unpleasant odor, perhaps from pet messes, sprinkle dry baking soda on the rug. Allow to set overnight, then vacuum. (Test for color fastness in an inconspicuous area.)

- Is the smell of your cat litter taking over your home? If so, cover the bottom of the litter pan with one part baking soda, then cover the baking soda with three parts litter to absorb odors for up to a week.

- Wooden cutting boards need to be disinfected occasionally. Scrub with a mild bleach solution, then rinse and rub the board with a thin coat of mineral or salad oil.

- To remove candle wax from a tablecloth, place the waxy section of the tablecloth between two thicknesses of paper toweling and press with a warm iron. If a greasy spot remains, treat it with a dry cleaning fluid.

- Hardened candle wax can be tough to remove from a candlestick! Try pouring boiling water into the candlestick socket to melt the wax. Once melted it should wipe out easily.

- Do you have white rings on your wooden furniture? These unsightly rings are often caused by setting down glasses without a coaster. Dampen a cloth with a small amount of mineral oil and dab it in fireplace ashes. Wipe gently on the ring, then polish or wax the wood as usual.

- It's always a good idea to save wallpaper scraps in case sections of the paper need to be repaired later. To make a patch, tear (don't cut) a scrap into the approximate size and shape needed. The irregular torn edges will blend better with the paper already on the wall, making the patch less apparent than if it had been cut.

- Here's an easy way to erase paint splatters from a brick fireplace. Get a broken brick the same color as the brick on the fireplace and scrub it back and forth over the spattered areas. Brick against brick will abrade away most of the paint. Any remaining paint will pick up the brick color and thus be camouflaged.

- Drapes can be sent out for cleaning, or, depending on their fabric, they could be washed. Once-a-year cleaning is generally enough.

- Miniblinds can be removed and hosed down with sudsy water and ammonia. Then they can be maintained monthly with a feather duster.

- Wash windows quarterly (more often if needed).

- Baseboards should be checked monthly and cleaned if needed.

- Check air conditioner/heating unit. The filters need to be checked and replaced at least twice a year. These must be kept clean for maximum efficiency and lowest cost.

- Barbecue grill can be scrubbed with a hard brush. Oven cleaner works well, but make sure to use rubber gloves. Remember to remove ashes after each use.

- Keep your awnings clean by scrubbing with a long-handled brush. Use water and a mild soap. Rinse with a hose. This is a great activity to get the kids involved in. Tell them to throw on their bathing suits and get to work!

- If you have unsightly oil stains on the cement drive-way or the floor of your garage, try scrubbing them out with detergent. Scrub with a stiff broom dipped in thick detergent suds. Repeat over the oil stains. Rinse by hosing down with clean water.

Paper Clutter Tips

Paper is here to stay, and it's a problem for almost everyone. Here are some quick tips for keeping the clutter to a minimum.

- Opt for e-mail statements for household bills whenever possible.

- Don't pile it, file it.
- Keep your shredder handy and always on ready for shredding. Try delegating shredding to an older child or neighborhood teenager looking to earn some money.
- When filing papers use categories and titles that you will remember.
- When pulling a file folder out of a drawer, place a sticky note in the place where it goes. Replacing the folder is a snap.
- Have a rule that when a new magazine or catalog arrives, the old one goes out.
- Read as much as possible online. Save important recipes and e-mails on your computer, instead of printing them out.

Preparation for Summer Safety

The National Safety Council estimates that more than half of all summer accidents could be prevented if people took simple, commonsense precautions. Summer brings varied schedules and activities: day and summer camp, skiing, swimming, biking, and many other activities which may result in animal bites, heat exposure, sunburn, cuts, insect bites, and much more. Unpredictable situations may be prevented by following these helpful hints:

- Post emergency phone numbers in plain view by the telephone for you and your children and the babysitter.
- Plan ahead by taking a first-aid class including CPR from your local Red Cross chapter. Many chapters offer the classes at no charge.
- Give your children swimming lessons at the earliest possible age. Many YMCAs offer great programs for children.

- If you are in an area where no swimming classes are offered, work with your children yourself. Start your children at a very young age by pouring water over their heads and having them hold their breath and blow bubbles underwater. Make it fun, and at the same time you will be helping them become comfortable in water.

- Common water-safety violations often result in injury. These include running, jumping, or sliding around a pool deck, diving without checking the water depth, swimming alone, and leaving a child unattended beside a pool, lake, or bathtub. Go over safety rules with the family *often*.

- Purchase (or put together yourself) a first-aid kit for car travel. Keep it handy for you but out of the reach of the children.

- Sunburn is very common, so use extra precautions. Sunscreen lotions are a must. Keep them handy for small children and light-skinned people, making sure to use at least SPF 30. A sun hat, visor, or bonnet is also recommended to prevent sunburned noses.

- Poison ivy, poison oak, and poison sumac are often found in uncultivated fields and wooded areas. Touching one of these plants (whose leaves often cluster three to a stalk) usually results hours later in an oozy, itchy rash that may spread over much of the body. The trouble comes with infection caused by scratching the area. If your summer plans include hiking or picnicking in wooded or mountain areas, review with the family the facts about these poisonous plants. You may want to go to the library and find photos of the plants. Ask questions and inquire about these and other potential dangers in the area you plan to go to. Educate yourself and your family for a safer outing.

- Insect bites or stings can cause swelling, pain, redness, burning, or itching which can last from 48 to 72 hours. If you know you are allergic to bee stings, before leaving town be sure to consult your doctor about any medication you may need to take along. This is a good item to keep in your first-aid kit.

- A honey bee leaves its stinger imbedded in the skin. It's best to remove the stinger with tweezers or by scraping with a fingernail. Wash the sting area with soap and water and apply ice or flush with cold water to reduce swelling and pain. It can also be relieved with Calamine lotion (available over the counter in drugstores) or by applying a paste of baking soda and water.

- Think ahead and plan ahead in order to be prepared for emergencies. When taking various foods on picnics, remember to keep the perishable items in coolers with lots of ice. Any food item containing mayonnaise is likely to go bad quickly. Don't let any food items sit in the hot sun. Eggs and uncooked meats need to be kept especially well-cooled.

- Take a car emergency kit. Some very good kits are available at auto parts stores. Or you can make up your own kit consisting of flares, jumper cables, a "HELP" sign, a "CALL POLICE" sign, a fire extinguisher, nylon rope, a towel, flashlights, fuses, and an approved empty gasoline can. All of these can be put together in a plastic dishpan, which can also be used to carry water in an emergency.

- Buy and use a "Hide-A-Key" box. This is a small box with an extremely strong magnet. Hide the spare key in the box and attach it to the car in a secret, hard-to-find area. (This makes an especially good gift for teen drivers.) Keys locked inside a car cause lots of trouble to lots of people. Think ahead to prevent this kind of trouble!

Getting Ready for Summer Fun

Summer is finally here and it's all about fun, vacations, and lots of outdoor activities! Help ready your home and yard for all you have planned.

- Set out your chairs and other backyard furniture for a quick cleaning. Spray with an all-purpose cleaner and hose off. Set them in the sun to dry.

- Purchase a few citronella candles to have on hand to burn while dining al fresco to keep those pesky bugs away.

- Purchase paper plates, cups, and napkins at the dollar store. They're so reasonable that you can use them often and keep cleanup to a minimum.

- When hosting a party and you need a place to ice down drinks, use your washing machine. Fill with ice and load up with drinks. When the party is over, simply let the ice melt and run the spin cycle to get rid of the water!

- Rub olive oil on your barbecue grill after cleaning to keep future cleanups to a minimum.

Preparing for Vacation Travel

Believe it or not, it can be a joy to travel with your children!

Granted, the preparation for a trip sometimes seems exhausting, and you may wonder if it is worth it all to leave the house, the pets, and a regular routine. But the excitement and wonder of children as they experience new sights will truly be an ample reward for the effort involved.

Here are some hints for making your trip smoother for the whole family.

- **Prepare your children for the exciting adventure.** Talk with them about where you are going and what you will be doing. As children grow out of the infant and toddler stages and as their world expands to include friends, some verbal preparation becomes very important.

- **Tell your youngsters about the fun that is in store for them.** Show them books, maps, and photographs about your route and destination. Be sure to reassure them that you will soon return home and that the toys they didn't take with them will still be there when they get back.

- **Watch your tendency to overpack.** The rule of thumb for experienced travelers applies to children as well: *Take just what you need and no more.* The length of the trip (adjusted for the dirt factor for your children) should give you a reasonable handle on the amount of clothing they will need each day. Bear in mind that a public Laundromat will probably be available during your travels.

- **Pack only clothing that your children like.** You don't want to deal with clothing battles on a long trip! Even a three-year-old can learn to help you pack. Lay out five items and let them choose two to take along. This is a great teaching tool. After your children become used to packing on their own, you can just take a moment to double-check their packing list and choices to be sure all the bases are covered.

- **Take toys that your children enjoy.** Again, let your child help in this area. A toy that you consider mundane might provide considerable amusement to your child. It's also a good idea to stash away a couple of new attention-getters—maybe a special surprise like a new toy that he or she has always wanted. But don't forget the tried and true, either. A special pillow, favorite blanket, cuddly stuffed teddy, or special doll are often comforting for a child sleeping in a strange bed for the first time.

- **Consider a backpack for the preschooler and older child.** This is a great way of limiting items or toys taken. Make a rule that your children can take along whatever fits into their backpack.

- **Bring along a surprise box.** Children love it when Mom and Dad have secrets for them. Your box can include such items as toys, food snacks, puzzles, books, and word games. Be creative but keep it a surprise, and when things get hectic or a child gets irritable, pull out the surprise box.

- **Plan frequent stops.** This is very important if you are traveling by car with small children. Cramped legs and fidgety children will be the cause of many arguments if not taken care of sensibly. Give your children plenty of opportunities to get out and run, skip, and jump for a few minutes, and also to use the restroom.

- **Always carry a small cooler with you.** Keep a cooler filled with milk, fruit juice, snacks, and fruit. This will be a pick-me-up, and the refreshment is always welcome. It will also prevent too many fast-food stops. Picnic whenever possible; it's cheaper and children love it.

- **Invest in a first-aid kit.** Fill an empty coffee can with Band-Aids, children's aspirin, antiseptic, thermometer, scissors, safety pins, tweezers, adhesive tape, gauze, and cotton balls. Try to cover all bases. Don't forget a good supply of handy wipes and a blanket.

- **Bring a flashlight.** Be sure to check the batteries before leaving home. When all else fails, children love to play with a flashlight. Take along an extra set of batteries.

- **Throw in your bathing suits.** Keep these in an easy-to-get-to place. Many motels and hotels have indoor pools that are usable even in the winter months. They may also have hot tubs or Jacuzzis. Also, you may find yourself stopping by a lake or beach for a quick swim.

- **Let your kids navigate.** Depending on the age of your children, give them a map so they can follow the route and tell you how far it is to the next stop or town. Older children can also keep a journal of the trip. Kids love to help navigate, and this will certainly cut down on the number of times you hear "Are we there yet?" from the backseat!

- **Send up a prayer for safety and patience.** Before we drive out of our driveway, we always offer a prayer for protection and patience. Prayer during the trips also helps to calm a tense situation.

Some of your most memorable times together as a family will come from traveling on vacation. With a little planning and preparation, those memories can be truly happy ones.

Travel Light

When you are traveling, don't take more luggage to the airport than you can carry yourself! If you can't carry it, you're taking too much. And clean out your purse or tote bag. There's at least a pound of stuff in there—receipts you don't need, ticket stubs, and loose change. Be sure you have some kind of expandable tote bag. You might as well count on having a place for all the souvenirs and gifts you plan to buy. Pack normally. Then take out half the clothes. Yep—half! And all those shoes? I don't think so! Lightening up every day is a great way to travel through your life journey too.

On a practical note, almost every airline is now charging

passengers for checked luggage. It's much cheaper and quicker to take carry-on luggage instead, even if it means leaving some desired items behind.

Garage Sale Tips

As summer comes to an end and you need something to keep your restless children busy, why not plan a garage sale? Tell them that they can keep the money from the sale of their items, and you'll be surprised at how quickly they get motivated to clean their rooms and get rid of all that clutter!

Not only will a garage sale tidy up your home, it can also be quite profitable. Our children often use their money to buy back-to-school supplies and new clothes. Another good idea is to give the money to a church project or a missionary family. After you help your children decide how they want to use the money they make, put on your grubbies, roll up your sleeves, and start planning.

The first step is to set your garage sale date. It is best to plan a one-day sale, either on a Friday or Saturday. Once that is set, call the newspaper or community shopper handout and place an advertisement.

Your ad should be short, to the point, and should *not* include your phone number. You don't need to answer a lot of phone calls and silly questions. Here is a sample ad:

Garage Sale
Saturday, Sept. 6, 9 a.m. to 5 p.m.
Bookcase—toys—antiques—
appliances—clothing—bike—tools
6256 Windemere Way

Make your signs using heavy cardboard or brightly colored poster board and bold felt pens in contrasting colors. Keep it simple. Merely write: "GARAGE SALE," the dates, your house address, and street name. Most people don't need too much prompting to drive by a garage sale. My car goes on automatic when it sees a garage sale sign, and stops dead-center in front of the house!

When placing your signs, make sure they are in a prominent location. Use your own stakes. Do not put them on top of a street sign or speed-limit sign. Always go back and remove your signs the day after your sale.

Make your decisions. Now comes the cleaning out and decision-making process. Spend time with each child going over the items they begin to pull out of their rooms. They sometimes get so excited that they want to sell their bed, favorite teddy bear, and even the dog or cat.

You'll have to watch yourself too. I (Emilie) got so excited at one of our garage sales that I sold our refrigerator! People were coming and buying so fast that I got all caught up in it. I didn't like our refrigerator anyway and thought a new one would be great. Besides, it looked like we were selling plenty and bringing in a lot of money. A couple asked me what else I had for sale and I said, "How about the refrigerator?" They bought it.

I was thrilled—until my husband, Bob, came home. I learned a good lesson: Keep your cool and don't lose your head!

Organize. Display items in categories. For example, put all the toys in one place, and glassware and kitchen utensils in another. Place breakable items on tables if possible.

Have an extension cord available from your garage or house outlet so people can check electrical appliances such as a popcorn popper, iron, electric razor, radio, or clock. If the item does not work, tell the truth. Your interested customer may still buy it. Many garage sale shoppers are handymen who can fix anything or can even use the parts from an appliance that no longer works!

Hospitality gives a garage sale an added touch. Try serving fresh coffee, tea, or iced tea.

Set your price. Pricing takes a lot of time and thought. As a general rule, keep your prices down. Never mark your price directly on the article. It is best to use stick-on labels, round stickers, or masking tape.

If individual family members are going to keep the money from the sale of particular items, be sure to mark them with appropriate initials or a color code (Linda has the blue label, Tom has the green).

Always price everything in increments of 50 cents—$1.50, $2.50, etc. That way you have some bargaining power. People love bargains.

It's also a good idea to have separate boxes containing items priced at 5 cents, 10 cents, and 25 cents. This will save you from having to mark each item separately. Children love these boxes because then they can shop while Mom and Dad look around. You can even have a box marked "FREE."

Have one person, preferably an adult, be the cashier, and accept only cash from your customers. All purchases must go through that person. Take a large sheet of poster board and list each person who is selling at your sale. As each item is sold, take off the price sticker and place it under his or her name or write the price in the appropriate column. At the end of the day, simply add up each column. This strategy is especially helpful if multiple families are participating in a neighborhood sale.

Make time count. On the day of the sale, get up early and commit the day to the sale. Eat a good breakfast; you'll need a clear mind for bargain decisions. Since people interested in antiques and valuable items will come by early, it is best to have everything set up the day before. Then all you have to do on the morning of the sale is to move your tables of items outside to the walkway, patio, or driveway.

Pack lunches the night before for you and your children. You won't have time to make lunch with people in your yard all day. Aim toward having a calm, loving spirit, and keep the family involved and available to help. Remember, this is a family project.

By the end of the day, you'll be ready for a hot bath and a chance to relax. Pop some popcorn, sit down with your family, and enjoy discussing the day's activities and the way you'll use your profits.

A Summer Memory Box

As the wonderful and warm days of summer are nearing an end, here's an idea to help you and your family transition back into the fall season.

Summer has likely been brimming with lazy, warm afternoons of swimming, biking, hiking, barbecuing, and a myriad of other fun activities. Vacations allowed for some amazing adventures and memories that will last through the year until next summer.

Don't trust your memory to recollect all the fun you had! Consider putting together a summer memory box. The box can be decorated by your children, or you and your husband can get involved and make it a family project. You can use the same box each summer or create a new box every year. Each family member should contribute items that will go into the memory box—pictures, seashells, ticket stubs, or postcards. It could include sand or rocks (in small containers, of course!) from that beach trip or your hike in the mountains. You might even encourage your school-aged children to write a brief story—complete with drawings—of their favorite summer moments. All of the items collected go into the memory box. Set it aside until summer is over and school is back in session. Once your children are settled into the school routine and back on a regular schedule, plan a family Summer Memory Night. Serve a summery meal, complete with lemonade, grilled burgers, and fruit salad! After dinner gather around the table or in your family room to reminisce about the wonderful summer you shared and all the memories. Go through the items in the box and take turns sharing the fun memories that made you smile!

Consider making this an annual tradition. It can help ease the ending of summer fun and the beginning of a very busy time of year. Create your own unique celebration and have lots of fun!

Fall Family Organization

Is getting the children organized a problem for you after a summer of irregular schedules? If so, start by planning a back-to-school organizational day with each child. For the working moms it may need to be a Saturday or an evening.

With a child, go through his or her drawers and closets and throw or give away summer clothing and outgrown shoes. A lot of the summer clothing can be stored away for next summer. Put clothing in boxes and label the boxes according to size, so when next summer arrives the clothing can be given to other members of the family or to friends whom they will fit. That way you can recycle your children's perfectly good clothes. The boxes can be stored in the basement, garage, attic, or closets.

If your child has grown over the summer, it might be time for some new clothes! For moms who sew, take the child with you when picking out patterns and fabrics. If you're shopping from mail-order catalogs, sit down and discuss the purchases with your child. Make it a togetherness time, and then he or she will feel part of the new wardrobe and the "I hate to wear that" syndrome will be eliminated. This method also teaches your children how to make decisions responsibly. Later on you'll find this guidance and time pay off as your children grow older and shop capably for themselves.

As you look at the new schedule for the fall, plan a family meeting to discuss home responsibilities. Make up a "Daily Work Planner Chart." Parents' names should also be listed on the chart. This shows that you work together as a family. Make a list of jobs the family can do to help around the house. Put each item on a separate piece of paper and put each into a basket. You may need two baskets, one for children's jobs 3 to 7 years old and one for children ages 8 to 18. Once a week, each child draws out two to five jobs. These jobs are put on the "Work Planner Chart."

As the children do their jobs, a happy face can be drawn by their name (or a sad face if they dropped the ball and neglected to do their job). Stickers or stars can also be used. This makes for a colorful chart.

If they complete their jobs easily, they may draw another job from the basket and get extra credit or double stickers, stars, or happy faces. Children become excited about duties around the house and work toward a colorful chart for each week of the month.

At the end of the month you can plan a special family surprise as a reward for jobs well done. You might say, "This month we've worked together as a family. Now we're going to play together as a family." Plan a fun Saturday bike ride ending with a picnic lunch or a Friday evening by the fire popping corn and playing a favorite family game.

Establish a Back-to-School Command Center

For a busy mom, having a successful school year is all about the ability to make the best use of your time. Many moms today work outside the home and time at home is precious. Before the school year begins, consider the advantage of having a "Back-to-School Command Center" where everything you need is at your fingertips. Purchase a large basket or plastic bin to store homework supplies, and your kids won't waste any more time looking for the items they need to complete a project! Set this bin in a place where it can be easily accessed each night. Remember: As Mom, you are the commander. The more efficient you are, the more time you'll save and have available for use on something much more worthwhile.

Store the following supplies in your homework center:

- File folders
- Accordion file—one for each child, color coordinated. These work great for holding paperwork and homework. Color-coding makes it easy to file and locate items quickly.
- Bulletin board (if you have room). Children can put up a list of their homework assignments and goals for the evening, or write the list on a whiteboard with dry-erase markers. They can cross off or erase each assignment as it's completed.

- Notepads, filler paper, and spiral notebooks
- Pens, pencils, crayons, colored pencils, markers, highlighters
- Calculator
- Pencil sharpener
- Ruler, compass, and protractor
- Glue stick
- Paper clips, stapler, hole punch
- Stamps, envelopes (different sizes)

It is great if you have a desk area that can be dedicated for this purpose, but even if you don't, you can place the items in a plastic roller storage container to be rolled out when needed. You and the kids will both save on stress when everything you need is handy!

The Busy Person's Thanksgiving Dinner

Today's busy women just don't have the time to do what great-grandma did. She cooked for days until Thanksgiving arrived. If the thought of roasting a turkey, cleaning the house, and getting the trimmings together for Thanksgiving dinner raises your stress level, then this bit of guidance should help. Apply these ideas to any holiday meal preparation.

Take a deep breath and think long enough to come up with a solution. For example, you can turn a stressful round of hosting a holiday meal into a potluck. Make a few phone calls and quickly organize a simple and delicious family meal.

First, develop your Thanksgiving dinner menu. Here is a sample menu:

> **Turkey, stuffing, cranberry sauce:** You will do this.
> **Beans:** Auntie Syd
> **Mashed potatoes:** Grandma Gertie
> **Rolls:** Uncle Blair

Relish dish: Brad
Pumpkin pie: Jenny

Phone your guests to invite them for a Busy Person's Thanksgiving Dinner. For your own reference, make a simple chart or list with their name and what item they will be bringing. (For example: Vegetable—Aunt Amy; Relish dish—Sue.) Ask them to RSVP at least ten days before Thanksgiving. This way you'll still have time to adjust things if someone can't make it after all.

As you plan, get your family involved. Assign the name cards to a child. Each card should have the name of a person and a Scripture verse inside. Each verse should pertain to thankfulness or gratitude. Before the meal, ask each person at the table to read his or her verse aloud.

Have another child make cards titled "I'm thankful for…" These should be given to your guests when they first arrive at your home, so they have time to think about their response.

After dinner each guest will read their thankful card. This is a great way to focus on the things God provides for us. Or you could have a child interview each guest, asking the question, "What is the best thing that has happened to you this year (month, week, today)?" This exercise has given our families many great memories and often brought tears from each of us.

Make out your grocery list for what you will need for the big day. As hostess you will be providing the turkey, stuffing, and cranberry sauce. A few days before Thanksgiving, make sure you have everything you will need for setting the table—including a centerpiece. Keep it simple by using a pumpkin surrounded by fresh fruit or three candles in autumn colors. (Votive candles floating in a glass or bowl of water also work well as a centerpiece.) To save time and money, try to use something you already have on hand.

Prepare your thawed turkey for roasting in the late afternoon on the day before Thanksgiving. I (Emilie) recommend my "Perfect Every Time" turkey recipe. I have found it to be a lifesaver for the busy woman. I've adapted the recipe from Adelle Davis's book *Let's Cook It Right* (New American Library, 1947). I've used this recipe for 45 years and never had it fail me yet!

Preheat oven to 350 degrees Fahrenheit.

Remove the neck and giblets and rinse turkey well. Dry turkey with paper towels, salt the cavity, and stuff with stuffing of your choice. Rub the outside of the turkey with olive oil. Stick a meat thermometer into the turkey.

Place the turkey breast-down in the roasting pan on a rack (this way the breast bastes itself, keeping the meat moist). Roast the turkey one hour at 350 degrees to destroy bacteria on the surface. Then adjust the heat to 180 or 200 degrees for any size turkey. The turkey can roast in the oven on this low temperature for 15 to 30 hours before you eat it. A good rule for timing is to allow about one hour per pound of meat. For example, a 20-pound turkey that takes 15 minutes per pound to roast would take 5 hours by the conventional, fast-cooking method. The slow method is 1 hour per pound, so it would take 20 hours to roast.

I usually begin roasting a 22-pound turkey at 5 p.m. on Thanksgiving Eve. I put the turkey in the oven and leave it uncovered until it's done the next day between 1 p.m. and 3 p.m.

Although the amount of cooking time seems startling at first, the meat turns out amazingly delicious, juicy, and tender. It slices beautifully, barely shrinks in size, and the vitamins and proteins are not harmed because of the low cooking temperature.

Once the turkey is done, it will not overcook. You can leave it in the oven an additional three to six hours and it will still not dry out. It browns perfectly and you'll get wonderful drippings for gravy.

Miracle Minutes for the Holidays

"Miracle Minutes" are simply using those five- or ten-minute blocks of time you can use to complete small, simple tasks around your home. Here is a list for the holidays:

- Take out your stemware, wash and dry.
- Iron any linens you will use on your holiday table.
- Dust one shelf of a bookcase or the fireplace mantel.
- Clean one mirror.
- Wipe out your silverware drawer.
- Go through your spices and get rid of ones that are more than three years old.
- Fill your decorative salt and pepper shakers for the holiday table.
- Write a "thinking of you" note to someone you love.
- Arrange Christmas cards attractively in a basket or on the mantel.
- Wrap one or two gifts.
- Replace videos and DVDs in their proper cases.
- Clean out the coffeepot by filling with an equal parts vinegar/water solution and turning it on. Run clear water through when you are done.

Blessings for a wonderful holiday!

Chapter 10

A Five-Week Plan of Action

Transformation in Just 15 Minutes a Day

Who wants to spend all their waking hours cleaning their home? Is there a way to live after a messy house? Yes. You don't have to be a slave to your home. Give me at least 15 minutes a day for five weeks and I can have you on top of the pile.

As with any task, you need some basic equipment:

- 3 large 30-gallon trash bags
- 3 to 12 large cardboard boxes (approximately 10" x 12" x 16"), preferably with lids
- 1 wide-tip black felt marking pen

Before you start this project, commit it to the Lord. Ask the Lord to provide you with the desire and energy to complete the project. In this program you will clean one room a week for five weeks. If you have fewer rooms it will take you less time and if you have a larger house it will take more than five weeks.

Start by designating the three trash bags as *put away, give away,* and *throw away.* Take these bags with you as you work through the house, starting at the front door and working your way back. Start with the hall closet and proceed through the living room, dining room, kitchen, bedrooms, and bathrooms.

A good rule to help you decide whether to keep an item is if you haven't used it for a year, it must be thrown away, given away, or stored away. Exceptions to this would be treasured keepsakes, photos, or very special things you'll want to pass down to your children someday.

Magazines, papers, scrap material, clothing, and extra dishes and pans must go.

As you pull these items off your shelves and out of your closets, they can be put into the appropriately labeled trash bags. What's left will be put back into the proper closet or drawer, or onto the proper shelf.

After the last room is finished, you will have at least three very fat trash bags. The throw-away bag goes out to the trash and the give-away bag can be divided up among needy friends or donated to a thrift store. The put-away bag will be the most fun of all! Take the large cardboard boxes and begin to use them for storage of the items you'll want to save for future use. Just *15 minutes a day* for five weeks has cleaned out all the clutter in your home!

Maintaining Your Five-Week Program

You now have your home clean—washed, dusted, sorted out, and painted through this Five-Week Program—and it feels good. Everything has a place in a cupboard, dresser, closet, or on a shelf; all your boxes are marked and properly filed away. Within a short time you can locate anything. Oh, that feels good. The pressure is off!

It's a big accomplishment, but you're not quite through. It's a matter of maintaining what you've worked so hard on the past five weeks. This is the easiest part when applied.

For this phase of your program you will need:

- One 3x5 file box
- 36 lined 3x5 file cards
- Seven divider tabs

Set-up your 3x5 file box with dividers. Label the dividers as follows:

- Daily
- Weekly
- Monthly
- Quarterly
- Biannually
- Annually
- Storage

Under each tab heading you now make a list of the jobs needing to be done on each file card. Some suggestions are:

- Daily
  - Wash dishes
  - Make beds
  - Sweep kitchen floor
  - Pick up rooms
  - Tidy bathrooms
  - Make preparations for dinner
- Weekly
  - Monday—wash
  - Tuesday—iron, water house plants
  - Wednesday—mop floor, dust
  - Thursday—vacuum, wipe down bathrooms
  - Friday—change bed linens
  - Saturday—yard work
  - Sunday—church, free
- Monthly
  - Week 1—Clean refrigerator and oven

- Week 2—Wash living room windows and bedroom windows
- Week 3—Mend clothing and clean bathrooms
- Week 4—Clean and dust baseboards; wax kitchen floor

• Quarterly
- Clean dresser drawers
- Clean out closets
- Move living room furniture and vacuum underneath
- Clean china cabinet glass
- Clean, rearrange, and organize cupboards in kitchen

• Biannually
- Hose off screens
- Change filter in furnace
- Rearrange furniture
- Clean garage, basement, or attic (schedule the whole family on this project)

• Annually
- Wash sheer curtains
- Clean drapes if needed
- Shampoo carpet
- Wash walls and woodwork
- Paint the paint chips or blisters on house

The above schedule is only a sample. Your particular projects can be inserted where needed. Living in different sections of our country will put different demands on your maintenance schedule. Get in the habit of staying on top of your schedule so you don't get buried again with your clutter and stress.

Emilie Barnes is the author of 70 books, including *The Twelve Teas® of Friendship; 101 Ways to Clean Out the Clutter; Heal My Heart, Lord;* and *15 Minutes Alone with God.* She appears on more than 300 radio stations as host of "Keep It Simple." Emilie and her husband, Bob, are also the founders of More Hours in My Day time-management seminars.

Sheri Torelli, author of the popular *The Fast-Food Kitchen,* is a nationally recognized conference speaker and owner/director of More Hours in My Day. Sheri and organization founder, Emilie Barnes, have worked together since 1981 to help women nurture their families and homes with simple steps. Together they coauthored the popular *More Hours in My Day.* Sheri and her husband, Tim, reside in Riverside, California.

To contact Emilie Barnes or Sheri Torelli, to find out more about More Hours in My Day time-management and organization seminars, or to buy More Hours in My Day products:

Write to:
More Hours In My Day
2150 Whitestone Drive
Riverside, CA 92506
(951) 682-4714

Visit:
Website: www.emiliebarnes.com

Or e-mail Sheri at:
sheri@emiliebarnes.com

MORE HOURS IN MY DAY: PROVEN WAYS TO ORGANIZE YOUR HOME, YOUR FAMILY, AND YOURSELF

For more than 25 years, Emilie and Sheri have conducted time-management seminars and taken the opportunity to listen to the thousands of attending women express their hearts' desires—to find more hours each day for what really matters most: family, home, and quality of life.

This book is their response. Here's a thorough collection of those time-tested answers to every woman's dilemma...

- Establish simple systems that save time and money and gain peace of mind
- Organize the home's problem areas—kitchen cupboards, crowded closets, home offices, and more
- Reclaim precious time for family and friends

Filled with inspiration, encouragement, and tried-and-true tips, this book is a must-have for every woman!

101 WAYS TO CLEAN OUT THE CLUTTER

Home management expert and bestselling author Emilie Barnes comes to the aid of every clutter keeper with 101 simple ideas to rid rooms of piles, stacks, and disarray. Readers will rediscover space and peace in their home as they

- stop making excuses for the useless items they keep
- eliminate junk mail before it junks up a drawer
- take back control over "stuff" and taste freedom
- subtract an item before adding an item
- reap the rewards of prioritizing time and space

Better than a how-to show, this compact resource can go anywhere a reader needs a little encouragement and lots of tips to transform clutter to cleaner at home, a friend's house, church, or the office.

THE FAST-FOOD KITCHEN:
GREAT MEALS AT HOME IN 15 MINUTES

Sheri Torelli, coauthor with Emilie Barnes of the popular *More Hours in My Day* (over 240,000 copies sold), presents a wonderful mealtime solution for families on the go, on a budget, and ready to switch from drive-through answers to fast, healthy, home-cooked meals.

Sheri provides realistic, fine-tuned ways to bring sanity and the family back to the table:

- double-duty cooking—how to maximize a minimal amount of time in the kitchen
- menus by design—foolproof ways to plan meals and a month's worth of menus
- creating little helpers—skill-appropriate tasks for kids of all ages
- tips for an efficient kitchen—tweaks and tools to organize a fast-food kitchen
- fast food with friends—hosting simple meals at home without feeling intimidated

This unique and practical resource provides the recipe for better eating and better living: meal plans, organization helps, and lots of encouragement.